# SHARPEN YOUR VERBAL EDGE

## 101 Tips to Enhance Your Professional Communication Skills

By Elizabeth MacDonald

**Sharpen Your Verbal Edge**
*By Elizabeth MacDonald*

ISBN: ?????????????????????????

Edited by Eli Gonzalez and Lil Barcaski
Book Design by Ymmy Marketing

Printed in USA

## Dedication:

I dedicate this book to my mother and hero Millie Nulf, whose positivity and zeal for life blesses and energizes whomever she's around and from whom I gleaned the importance of words, vocabulary-building, and using correct grammar and punctuation.

My mother models a life steeped in love, service to others, and encouragement.

As you approach your 100th birthday, Mom, know that your legacy lives on in your family and in this book.

I love you!

# Table of Contents

# Foreword

When I first met Elizabeth, and she explained her business, I became somewhat self-conscious of my word choices not wanting to use "wasteful" or "throw away" words and leaning into her vast knowledge and expertise wanting to know more. I shared with Elizabeth that many people, including myself, might be intimidated by her passionate zeal to help people become better and more engaging communicators.

As the President and CEO of a community-based technology park and dynamic entrepreneurial community, on a 55-acre campus, adjacent to several educational institutions in Northeast Indiana, our campus epitomizes an active learning community. Over the last eighteen years, I have served the organization, I have had the opportunity to work and learn, all over the world, from thousands of entrepreneurs, innovators, business builders, dreamers and solopreneurs. Moreover, I have thoroughly enjoyed coaching and mentoring Elizabeth, and in the process, she has taught me a valuable lesson that I reflect on often. She models for each of us what we should want and demand ourselves: to be vulnerable, to aim higher and to discover and realize our individual human potential.

Over the years, I have had the privilege and opportunity to learn, discover, laugh and grow with Elizabeth. She is a special person with rare talents. She projects confidence, positivity, and energy in her relationship-building, and she puts joy and meaning into her connections to others. She absorbs new knowledge and business insights like a sponge. She continually risks herself, makes herself vulnerable, and actively applies her personal discoveries and learnings. She is "all in" in helping others overcome their communications fears and challenges.

We can all acknowledge that purposeful and intentional communications are at the hallmark of an effective communicator. At times, each of us has had a fear of public speaking or experienced a near miss in the delivery of critical information to a small group or a large crowd. Now, there is no reason why you cannot be a better version of yourself: a more effective and capable communicator — with the powerful tools, insights, and techniques that Elizabeth offers in her book.

Elizabeth reminds us all of the need to choose our words carefully, the sheer power of our word choices in defining our individual communication's style, and how to make a memorable and lasting first impression. By paying attention to her communication rules and practicing them in your daily interactions with others, you too can be a more effective and powerful communicator activating more exceptional career and life choices and, in the end, realizing what Henry David Thoreau opined, "**Go confidently in the direction of your dreams! Live the life you've imagined.**" With Elizabeth's commonsense rules, useful frameworks and practical tools, you too can imagine passing the invisible boundaries standing in your way, and, in the end, realizing many more "memorable and sticky" communication moments.

**Karl R. LaPan**

President and CEO

The Northeast Indiana Innovation Center, Inc.

# Introduction

You're reading this book because you want to improve your writing, speaking, and interpersonal relationship skills.

Like my clients and those who have read these tips, which I've posted over the years, you are most likely a good communicator who is striving to be even better! You are THE person I'm thinking of as I write this.

Welcome to a tip-by-tip journey to a more confident and effective way to present yourself and your message!

As we walk through these tips together—in whatever order you desire—you'll experience my passion and commitment to communication skills. My hope is you'll be drawn to these tips, learn them, practice them, and own them.

I strive to enhance my communication skills daily—I'll share some of the ways through my tips—and I'll be pushing you to do the same.

Because your reading this, I know you'll agree that intentionally clear, succinct, respectful, and situation-appropriate communication skills—verbal and non-verbal—are essential to our successfully conveying who we are, how we think, and what we stand for.

I am a speaker, communication skills advisor, and owner of The Verbal Edge. I give customized workshops and consultations to groups and individuals.

This book contains much of what I cover in those workshops and consultations: presentation skills; positive, clear, diplomatic, confidence-exuding communication; elimination of verbal clutter and fillers; effective email writing and formatting; advanced networking; active listening: vocabulary-building; and grammar and punctuation reminders.

I am passionate about these skills and began honing them before founding The Verbal Edge—thanks to my previous invaluable careers:

- TV broadcasting: anchoring, reporting, hosting talk shows, and producing those shows and newscasts
- Communication specialist for a large school district
- High school English teacher

Teaching high school English ignited my passion for helping others communicate better and is the inspiration for what I do now with my professional clients and why I've written this book.

Here is the situation I faced in the classrooms and the miraculous outcome:

On the first day of school, many of my spirited students stated they liked the way they spoke and initially dismissed the importance of speaking and writing correctly. At the end of the school year, my sophomores were crafting well-written papers and were oblivious to the impressive, vast vocabulary they had amassed. I had immersed them in an environment where we all excitedly delighted in daily transforming problem-packed and content-glutted sentences into succinct masterpieces. I also taught a concept word each day, and they used it immediately—creating, and then reading aloud, sentences containing that word and previous words-of-the-day. And to expand their vocabulary even further, they teamed up to create several more words from lists of prefixes and roots I provided each week. What also drove this last activity were the fun-sized Snickers bars I awarded to the two groups who created the most words that week!

Immersing my students in these communication skills was a life-changing experience for them and me. Out of that came The Verbal Edge, which equips professionals to effectively present, write, and speak with confidence. Through consultations and workshops, I now get to teach people who—from the start—want to improve their communication skills and can immediately apply what they learn.

For you, this collection of tips represents a gift of a lifetime of knowledge in verbal and non-verbal skills. These tips will equip you to be even more confident when presenting yourself —whether you speak in front of a group, interview or are the interviewer, host or attend video conferences, or need to polish your writing skills

I'm excited to share them with you.

Let's get started!

# SECTION 1

# The Importance of Communication Skills

You have something important to say. You want people to focus on it, remember it, see you as a trustworthy expert, and feel positively toward you.

That's what you'll explore in this section, which provides the foundation for the rest of your communication-skills journey.

I have selected these and all the tips in this book from professional situations I have witnessed, successful approaches I've learned, and topics I teach. For those reasons, you'll notice some of the tips, examples, or situations surrounding them may be different from what you would expect. Sound intriguing? I hope so!

Now let's start with focusing on the essential concept: Communication skills themselves.

# 1. Communication Skills Can Make or Break Your Career

How important are communication skills?

According to training development specialist Shirly Fine Lee, when people are terminated, 80% of the time, it is because of their lack of leadership or people skills.

Here's where it gets interesting: 80% of people are hired because of their competencies. Many times, competencies can be taught after a person is hired; however, when people come on board with subpar communication skills, those inadequacies eventually surface and unforeseen challenges arise. One option is coaching or training in those areas. Without intervention, companies are left to deal with people who may be unable to:

- Give positive and effective corrective feedback.
- Diplomatically and effectively approach or converse with colleagues, team members, bosses, and clients.
- Actively listen and engage.
- Format and write effective, practical, and powerful business emails.
- Give confident presentations to large or small groups.

In this book, you'll have the benefit of mini-lessons that address these topics and will propel you even further in your communication skills and give you The Verbal Edge.

Enjoy the process!

## 2. Maintaining Top-notch Communication Skills

Achieving and maintaining top-notch communication skills is an ongoing process.

Here are some suggestions:

- Continually read books and articles focused on improving communication skills. (Thank you for adding this one to your library!)
- Read well-written books and articles and pay attention to exemplary sentences and phrases.
- Listen to and watch riveting presenters—and take notes.
- Attend communication skills workshops.
- Hire a communication skills coach.
- Seek out accountability partners to point out your grammar mistakes and verbal clutter.
- Ask to have your correspondence proofread—and return the favor.
- Join toastmasters.
- Start blogging and writing.
- Ask for feedback and respond with gratitude.

# SECTION 2

# Presenting Yourself and Your Message

The tips in this section will give you that all-inclusive edge at pulling off a great first impression that lasts.

You'll have the edge in video conferencing because you and your background look perfect. My years in broadcasting provides the framework for these suggestions, some of which will surprise you.

You'll have the edge in presenting because you will have provided the person who introduces you with a short introduction that not only tells the audience why they should care about the topic but also why you are the ideal person to present it.

You will have the edge with your audience and others because your body language exudes confidence and positivity.

And you will have The Verbal Edge because of the professional words you use in addressing others—audience members, clients via video conference, people with whom you network, and recipients of your emails.

In this section and continuing throughout the book, most of the examples lean toward the business world. However, everything you'll learn is transferable to situations at home, in school, at parties, hosting webinars, and wherever you want to effectively and respectfully connect with others.

## BEFORE YOU SPEAK – PREPARE
## THE ENVIRONMENT AND THE CONTEXT

### 3. Video Conferencing, Part 1

How to come across as credible and professional when video conferencing—tips gleaned from my many years in broadcasting.

- Get close to the camera lens. You want a tighter shot. Video is a personal medium and we want you near us during this conversation and not, seemingly, across the room.

- Frame your face so your eyes are in the upper third of the screen. If done correctly, the closer you are to the screen, the less headroom you will have. Why do this? If your eyes are in the middle of the screenshot or below, your viewers will subconsciously perceive you— and your message—as less important and credible.

- Look straight into the lens. Arrange your computer or mobile device so that lens is at eye level—and look at that lens. Usually, this means elevating your computer quite a bit. Viewers don't want to see us looking down the whole time... and they don't want to see our ceilings.

- Avoid light backgrounds—windows, light walls, bright lamps, if outside—white cloudy skies. Cameras automatically adjust for bright light, and the result is everything else darkens—including our faces. So, choose a darker background, and you'll be amazed at how visible you'll become! Darker complexioned people need to be especially aware of this.

Also, sit or stand where light—artificial or natural—illuminates your face.

In the next tip, we'll focus more on what's behind us as we set the stage for our professional video conferencing shots.

## 4. Video Conferencing, Part 2

You're about to initiate or be involved in a video meeting. In addition to your words, content, and demeanor, you will need to know how to, literally, set the stage. This is crucial.

In my last tip, I covered how to frame yourself in the shot, light your face, look at the camera's lens, and place the lens at eye-level by elevating your computer or tablet.

This time, we're zeroing in on your background:

- Make sure no plants, lamps, or poles "grow out of your head." Either move the items a little or change the angle of your computer.

- Get rid of those cardboard boxes that are on the floor in the distance. We see them. And we see any other mess or clutter behind you.

- Look at what's displayed on your walls and bookshelves. Is it distracting? Is it inconsistent with your branding / what you want to convey?

- Dim any bright lights behind you and close the blinds/curtains if it's daylight unless you want to be seen in silhouette.

- If you're in front of a plain wall, sit/stand at least a couple of feet away from it unless you're striving for the mug-shot effect.

Video conferencing is a learning experience: I suggest you practice with someone beforehand.

What else have you seen or experienced that distracted or confused you?

## 5. Write the Introduction to Your Presentation

Have you ever sat through a presentation wondering who the speaker is, why that person was chosen, what the message is, and why you should care?

I have.

That information needs to be clearly stated in the introduction.

When I present, I write an introduction, email it beforehand, and take a copy with me—written in a large font so the person introducing me can easily read it.

An introduction is not a bio. It needs to be short and engaging as well as informative.

When writing your introduction, think SIN—David Greenberg uses that acronym in his book, *Simply Speaking!*

- S: Subject/title of the presentation
- I: Importance: Why the subject is important to the audience and why you are important to the topic (credibility)
- N: Your name.

I tell my clients to even write the last line. Say something like "Let's welcome..." That way, the person doing the introduction won't resort to the cliché "Without further ado" which means "without further messing around/confusion," which, ironically, disparages both the topic and the presenter!

## FIRST IMPRESSIONS

## 6.   The Power of a Smile

I had the privilege of giving a college commencement address. My topic: "10 Essential Communication Skills for a Successful Career."

Topping that list: SMILE.

Smiling communicates confidence. It is contagious. It attracts people to us and, instantly, they feel positive about themselves and us, the situation, and our message.

How positive? A smile causes the release of the same number of endorphins—chemicals that make us feel good—as eating 2,000 chocolate candy bars or receiving the equivalent of nearly $25,000 in cash. Those statistics are according to Katerina Nikolas, author of "How Smiling Affects Your Health."

Ron Gutman, author of *Smile: The Astonishing Powers of a Simple Act* says, "Smiling also makes us look more friendly and easy to approach... we seem more likable, friendly, sociable, courteous, and polite.

So, make a positive, confident difference in yourself, and others: smile.

## 7. Making That Great First Impression on Your Audience

When speakers appear uncertain, their listeners doubt their credibility, remain unconvinced, and struggle to relate.

Our audiences or those we need to impress for those all-important meetings can instantly detect this.

So, to exude confidence and positivity, we need to:

- Be professionally and appropriately attired—dress a notch above the audience.
- Prepare and rehearse.
- Stride up to the lectern with erect posture.
- Smile.
- Off to the side of the lectern, firmly shake the hand of the person who just introduced you.
- At the lectern, arrange your papers, look up, smile, and begin.
- Look AT the people in the audience—not above, as some people recommend.
- Refrain from touching your face, swaying, walking continually back and forth, speeding through your delivery.
- Gesture widely.
- Enjoy the experience—the audience will feel that.
- Get the audience involved right away. But don't insult them. (More on that in the next tip.)
- Eliminate confidence-robbing words and replace them with confidence-exuding words and intentional pauses—more on that later.

## 8. Avoid Alienating Your Audience

Will he or won't he insult his audience?

I held my breath after the new assistant pastor enthusiastically began his message with "Good morning."

This is where so many speakers wait for a reply, and if the group reply is not to the speakers' liking, they say something like, "You can do better than that!" And then they repeat, "Good morning" and expect a louder, more energetic response.

I've also heard speakers say, "How is everybody?" and then admonish the audience if the response is too low on the robust-meter.

To my relief, this young man did not do that. After saying "Good Morning," he launched right into his message. The congregation immediately connected, and that connection deepened because, within a couple of minutes, he complimented them.

That wasn't the case at a day-long seminar I attended a few months later. The first speaker wanted to set the tone, so she shouted, "Good morning" and waited for our response. Evidently, we weren't loud and energetic enough, so she shouted "Good morning" two more times!

The irony is that our third response was the weakest—a clear message to the speaker to back off!

My advice to speakers: Strive to connect, build rapport, and don't alienate and insult. We audience members have come to learn and may not be ready immediately to enthusiastically respond on demand—and that from a speaker who is also a morning person and an extrovert!

## 9. Making That Great First Impression on Your Client

In business, a positive first impression is essential.

Here is how you pull it off: You are at a restaurant and you're meeting a new client for the first time. The client walks toward your table and you:

- Smile.

- Stand (This applies to women also - Business is gender-neutral.)

- Begin and maintain eye contact.

- Greet the person by name.

- Confidently introduce yourself, if the person does not know you.

- Firmly shake the person's hand—web to web. (That's a Karen Hickman* term, and I like it. It means you move your hand all the way into the other person's hand until the webbing between your thumb and pointer finger touches their webbing.)

- Sit with a straight posture. Lean in when appropriate to show engagement.

- When addressing the client throughout the meeting, turn your upper torso toward the person. This conveys you are giving him/her your total attention.

- Keep your hands away from your face. Besides being a distraction and a barrier, your hands obstruct your mouth, which many hard-of-hearing people focus on to help decipher communication. Keeping your hands away from your face is also essential if background music is playing or other people are talking.

- If using laptops, be sensitive to the fact that monitors are also barriers, so arrange them accordingly and close the monitors when not using them.

*Karen is an etiquette consultant. Her company is Professional Courtesy.

## 10. How You Eat and Interact at Lunch Speaks Volumes.

Perhaps, you're meeting a prospective client, or you're in the final stages of an interview for "the best job ever," and that interview involves lunch.

What you do—how you handle yourself and how you eat—is as important as what you say! That other person may not intend to scrutinize your table manners; however, if you unknowingly do something that is questionable, you now have their attention.

Here is what you do before, during, and after that lunch/dinner:

- If you are the first to arrive, stand to greet the other person/people when they arrive. This pertains to women as well. The business world is gender-neutral.

- Place your napkin in your lap. (I know, 99% of you would do this. To that 1%, PLEASE make this a habit—starting today.)

- Keep your hands away from your face—this applies to all meetings you attend. If you habitually cover your mouth—partially or completely, you obstruct your communication. And in restaurants, because of the ambient background music and conversations, more people need to read lips.

- If you need help pushing food onto your fork, use your knife or a piece of bread—NEVER your fingers. Imagine what that communicates about you and the cleanliness of your fingers!

- Don't cut all your meat at once. Gone are the days that someone did that for you, so they could get back to eating their food. Cut just the piece you are going to eat. I had lunch with someone recently who diced her entire serving of spaghetti before taking her first bite. I thought that was strange.

- Be polite to the server. Your prospects or prospective boss is watching how you treat other people.

- Judge what to order from what your host orders.

- Not everything needs ketchup or salt. Taste the food first. It may be an insult to smother something in ketchup—especially an expensive steak paid for by someone else.

- Chew with your mouth closed.

- Don't talk until you have swallowed. You can indicate that it will be a few seconds before you can respond. People understand and appreciate that gesture.

- By the way, if you invited the prospective client, you are expected to pay for the meal.

Many more etiquette rules/suggestions exist. I recommend you research them, embrace them, and champion them.

## 11. Interviewing: Attire and Demeanor

Can our attire and demeanor pass the test?

A young friend of mine had an interview at a temp agency. He was applying for a factory job.

I knew him well enough to be familiar with his wardrobe, so I encouraged him to wear a pressed long-sleeved shirt, his black pants, black belt, and black shoes.

Before the interview, we role-played and focused on the handshake and his introducing himself. After the interview, as part of the procedure, the young man was drug tested.

He failed the test. The test showed he had cocaine in his system. However, because of his appearance and the way he handled himself, the agency retested him.

This time, he passed. (The first drug test had shown a FALSE positive.)

The person interviewing him told me later that she retested him because of the way he spoke, acted, and dressed.

The way we dress tells others what we think about ourselves, the situation, and the people to whom we are speaking.

# ARE YOUR EMAILS AND TEXTS PROFESSIONAL AND EFFECTIVE?

## 12. Writing and Formatting Professional Emails, Part 1

Most professional emails are skimmed. People want to quickly find the relevant information. And many times, because of large paragraphs and superfluous information, they miss it.

The solution is to be succinct, on-topic, clear, and provide white space.

Here are some essential tips to ensure your email recipients read what you want them to:

- Subject lines: Write them as headlines: specific and information rich. They are key to whether our emails are even opened! (Think of people on mobile phones in rapid-delete mode.)

  Examples:

  - Company picnic rescheduled (not: picnic or hi)
  - Acme project update (not: project)
  - Recommended content for Tom's presentation (not: presentation)
  - Last day to order conference tickets (not: Tickets or Ordering)

- First sentence: It needs to further clarify the subject line. This is not the place for:

  - "How are you?" (Remember, these are professional

emails that you want opened and read.)

- – "I just want to write and say." (These are superfluous words. Just say it.)
- – "It is recommended by me that..." (Say, "I recommend..." The reader doesn't have time to figure out who is doing what.)

- Use simple language. A *Boomerang* study discovered that emails written at a 3rd grade level garnered the most responses.

- Use positively-constructed words. (See "Changing Negatives to Positives" in this book.) Negatively-constructed sentences confuse and, many times, needlessly upset readers:

  - – Instead of saying, "Don't forget..." say, "Remember to..."
  - – Instead of saying, "We can't wait to see you..." say, "We are eager to see you."

Go right to the next tip to read the rest of my recommendations.

## 13. Writing and Formatting Professional Emails, Part 2

Continuing with ways you can ensure your emails are clear, effective, and read:

- Be generous with your paragraphing and double space between them:
  - Create a new paragraph for any subtle change in topic or idea. This helps the reader organize the information.
  - Double spacing creates white space that easily guides your hurried reader to each important nuance or detail.
- Use bullet points. They:
  - Condense and organize information.
  - Create even more eye-friendly white space.
- Include a greeting (also known as a salutation) and a close (also known as a complimentary close). All professional emails need to include them for clarity and personalization:

  Salutation examples:
  - Good morning Team,
  - John,
  - Hello John,

  Complimentary close examples: (Check out the internet for lists of closes.)
  - Thank you,
  - Appreciatively,
  - Looking forward to hearing from you,

- Type your first name under the close—even though your name is included in your signature block. And please DO include your signature block! That's the professional way to end a letter, and your readers need that information.

- If a conversation thread develops, you do not need to continue starting with a greeting and signing your name. However, if you email that person or group later in the day on a different topic, you, once again, include the greeting and close along with your signature.

- Proofread, proofread, proofread. Your grammar and punctuation need to be correct.

## 14. Writing and Formatting Professional Texts

Treat professional texts in much the same way as emails:

- Start with the greeting: type the person's name followed by a comma.
- On the next line, begin your message.
- Close with your name typed on a separate line.
  - Example:

    Pat,

    Are you able to meet for lunch at 11:30 instead of noon?

    Let me know before 10:00 today.

    Thank you,

    Elizabeth
- Unlike email formatting, text formatting is more relaxed and complimentary closes are optional. (The example above shows a complimentary close. I always include one in my initial texts to clients, prospects, colleagues, and others with whom I am transacting business.)
- Spell out the words in your texts and avoid jargon unless you are texting someone in your industry. For some people, LOL means "Lots of love."
- Punctuate! Capitalize, add commas and periods. Remember, these are professional texts and people are forming opinions about you and your company.
- Start a new paragraph with every new idea instead of packing all the information into one endless paragraph.
  - You don't need to double space between paragraphs as you do in emails. Just giving your

new topic its own line alerts the reader to a change. I do encourage you to double space between unrelated topics.

- – Remember, you want to help your reader by visually organizing your message as much as possible.

- Treat conversation threads the same way you treat email conversation threads: You don't need to start with the person's name or end with yours.

- – However, in most cases, I encourage you to continue to do so in case you mistakenly send the text to another client, etc. (It happens!)

We are focusing on professional texts. However, many friends, family members, and acquaintances appreciate receiving texts that are well written, correctly punctuated, and jargon-free. Everything we do makes an impression on others. Texts that display our ability to write well reinforce the positive impression we want to foster. And that impression could lead to business referrals.

# SECTION 3

# Choose the Right Words

Every week, when I taught high school, I divided my students into groups, gave them five root words and five prefixes, challenged them to assemble as many actual words as they could, and then had them teach those words to the rest of us. The two groups with the most words got Snickers bars—the quintessential reward.

My students loved the investigative part, and it didn't stop there. On standardized tests and in their reading, they started encountering words whose meanings they could now easily figure out.

They realized this: To choose the right words, we must know their meaning. And discovering the logic to the word's construction—the etymology—is like identifying and choosing those puzzle pieces that reveal the picture.

Building your vocabulary is essential. This section contains some tips—and nudges—that will help.

Also, in this section, you'll become aware of how indifference toward words can produce misunderstanding, misuse, and mistakes.

After reading this section, you'll notice how easily you tackle verbal challenges—and others will notice also!

## BUILD YOUR VOCABULARY

### 15. Systematically Increase Your Vocabulary

Do you need a reason to increase your daily vocabulary?

Anthony Robbins, in the article "Change Your Words, Change Your Life," says, "According to Compton's Encyclopedia, the English language contains some 500,000 words. Yet the average person's working vocabulary consists of 2,000 words: 0.5% of the entire language. And the number of words we use most frequently—the words that make up our habitual vocabulary... averages 200-300 words."

I recommend this method to increase daily vocabulary usage:

- When you hear or read words you haven't used for a while, write them in your journal or enter them in your mobile device. I title my list "Vocabulary." Update it often.

- Choose five of those words and use them throughout the week.

- To reinforce your using them, rehearse. Say or write sentences containing the words before you debut them.

- Each week choose five more words.

- Record the list and play it in its entirety while exercising, driving, etc.

- Stop the recording after every 2-3 words and create sentences for those words.

- Bonus suggestion: Find an accountability partner to do this with you.

It works! And instead of being tempted to repeat mindless, knee-jerk words, which are at the top of all of our minds because we constantly hear them, you can be INTENTIONAL and use the appropriate word for the situation.

Make this a priority, and the number of your previously-unused or seldom-used words will skyrocket!

## 16. **Go for Exponential Vocabulary Growth:**

Each root word we learn greatly boosts our vocabulary and reinforces the meanings of all those new words.

Let's look at just one root word. You'll be amazed what you'll learn in the next minute! (By the way, that's an embedded positive command.)

Let's explore and inspect the root word SPEC: to SEE.

- Spectacle: anything we SEE that is impressive
- Spectacles: What we SEE with
- Spectacular: BEAUTIFUL in a dramatic EYE-CATCHING way; impressive, PICTURESQUE; An impressive, large-scale spectacle/DISPLAY
  - A song is not spectacular.
  - A show featuring music enhanced with dancers, brilliant flashing lights, fog, and revolving scenery could be spectacular.
- Specimen: (in microbiology, etc.) a sample of a substance or material for EXAMINATION or study.
- Speculation:
  the contemplation or consideration of some subject: (What one ENVISIONS)
- Specious: something that LOOKS factual or real but is fallacious or misleading.
- Respect: to SHOW regard or consideration for

As we inspect (LOOK carefully at) these words, we see the role "spec" plays.

In retrospect (LOOKING back), I could have added at least ten more words.

See how much fun this is?! Now do the same with more root words. Look up lists of root words on the internet, combine them with prefixes, and go for it! You'll be amazed at how words you've taken for granted were intentionally constructed to say exactly what they say!

Definition references are from the Random House Dictionary, © Random House, Inc. 2018.

## TOSS THE CRUTCH WORDS

### 17. Eliminate "very" and "really"

Let's stretch our vocabulary. And let's do it by eliminating the qualifier words "very" and "really" and choosing the precise word.

For example, instead of saying:

- "really easy," you could say, simple, effortless, painless, feasible, uncomplicated, a snap.
- "very interesting," say, intriguing, compelling, fascinating, absorbing, provocative, captivating, engaging.

Make diving into the thesaurus an essential process of your writing and you'll hear the results in your speaking.

If you feel ambitious, how about also eliminating the word "pretty" (as in "pretty tasty")?

To read more on eliminating qualifiers, check out "This is Pretty Interesting," my article on www.TheVerbalEdge.com.

"Really" does not mean "very." They are not synonyms. "Really" means actually, truly, or indeed. If you say, "The movie was really good." You are saying, "The movie was actually good."

Now, back to the word "very." I recommend my clients refrain from using it. "Very" allows the speaker/writer to mentally coast by selecting a favorite stand-by adjective and bolstering it with "very."

The movie was more than very good. It might have been intriguing, or spell-binding, cathartic, suspenseful, mesmerizing, life-changing, etc.

Listeners/readers will appreciate the effort and results of this precise communication.

They really will.

# 18. Absolute Words Want to (Absolutely) Stand Alone

If you declare you want your writing or speaking to be "absolutely excellent," expect to be challenged.

By saying "absolutely excellent," you have attempted to upgrade a word—excellent—that is non-gradable. You are tampering with an absolute adjective.

Absolute adjectives are complete in themselves. They embody 100% of the meaning. They don't need our help. So, qualifiers such as "very" and "less" are useless and confusing.

Something cannot be very excellent, less excellent, more excellent, or extremely excellent. It's either excellent, or it isn't. And if it isn't, then we need to choose words that are not absolute adjectives. (It's flawed, appealing, popular, desirable, or striking.)

Here are some other absolute adjectives. (Many more exist). Put them to the "very, less, more" test and you'll see what I mean:

| dead | essential | fatal | entire | complete |
| pregnant | freezing | square | whole | ultimate |
| impossible | brilliant | unique | irrevocable | empty |

Here is a sentence containing several absolute adjectives:

"Even though Ben was exhausted because of his packed schedule, he volunteered to clean the enormous gym, so it would be spotless for the final game."

Now, reread the above sentence and insert "very" before exhausted, packed, enormous, spotless, and final. See how that qualifier diminishes the meaning, integrity, and importance of all of those words? Now reread the original sentence again. Can you appreciate that each of those words had a job to do, and did it?

When we use absolute adjectives without attempting to vary them in intensity, it shows we understand and respect the meaning of those words and have the confidence to use them appropriately. And people notice.

This communication tip is essential for those who aspire to be excellent writers and/or speakers.

## 19. Resist the Temptation to Tag These Words with "up, out, back," etc.

Despite our inclination—even determination—to assist the following words, they are fully-equipped to stand alone: Switch, swap, report, and revert. They (and many others) contain their whole meanings. So, to follow them with words such as UP, OUT, and BACK is to render them redundant and confusing.

For example:

Many people are now saying swap OUT. "Swap" means to exchange, substitute, or replace one thing for another. The definition includes the concept of taking something out and putting something else in. So, if we say swap OUT, we are saying take something out and replace it with something OUT. What!?

Switch and swap have similar meanings. So, the same convoluted communication occurs with switch OUT and switch UP. Just say switch. And how about separate OUT? Please just say separate.

Because I was a reporter, I'm including report BACK. "Port" means to carry and "re" means back. So, when we say report BACK, we're saying carry information back BACK. Just say report.

The same applies to revert BACK. "Vert" means to turn and "re" means back. So, when we say revert back, we're saying turn back BACK. Just say revert.

I could list (not list out!) a myriad of examples.

What other superfluous combinations come to mind?

## ESCHEW FAUX PAS AND CONFUSIONS

### 20. Trade the Ambiguous for the Precise:

Are you using ambiguous or knee-jerk words that are open to your listener's interpretation? And do you know what they mean or are you guessing?

Here is why I ask:

While doing a workshop in the Tampa Bay area, I asked participants to rank the word "awesome" on a 5-point scale.

Awesome describes anything that is jaw-dropping—that elicits awe. It could be something magnificent or horrendous. And it is indisputably a 5 on the 5-point scale.

Or so I thought until one of the groups at the workshop ranked "awesome" as a 2. Those participants were in their 20s and said the word means "so-so."

The participants admitted they had never looked up the definition. They surmised the meaning by listening to the contexts in which other people used the word. ("Awesome pencil.")

So, when we use words such as "awesome" or "cool" as generic catch-all words, we are at the mercy of the other person's definition and we've abdicated our role as communicator to the other person.

Here's an example:

A client suggested we meet at his favorite coffee shop for a consultation. He described the coffee shop as "pretty cool." With only that to go on, I envisioned the place as rustic and cozy—but not too rustic and cozy because he used the qualifier "pretty." (If you're questioning why "pretty" is a diminishing qualifier, think of the phrases "pretty truthful" or "pretty accurate.")

Back to the story: When I arrived at the coffee shop, I was surprised to walk into a cavernous room that contained stainless steel chairs and tables. I shared my expectations with my client, who immediately decided to stop using that phrase.

He realized that to accurately convey his thoughts, he needed to choose the precise words instead of top-of-the-mind generic adjectives.

## 21. Are You Sure You Want That Word to Modify All the Others?

Be vigilant of your word order!

Have you ever started reading a seemingly mundane list and ended up thinking, *that is bizarre!*?

I have. And I've inadvertently created the same type of bizarreness.

We do it when we assign an adjective to the first word in the list and our readers, understandably, attach that adjective to all the other words in the list.

Here are some examples:

- The groom sat beside his annoying neighbor, bride, and family.

- The newspaper article featured the neighbors' uniquely-constructed house, marriage, and children.

- I have enclosed my photoshopped picture, birth certificate, and $40 check.

- Enjoy your pre-approved business classes, dorm, and friends.

- The corporation's entrance has massive columns, statues, and doormen.

- On her first day at work as an interior designer, Jayla's schedule included time set aside for her passion: color selection, her boss, and filling out human resources forms.

Before looking at how I've re-structured the sentences so they make more sense, review them and figure out what changes you would make.

Here are some options that clear up the miscommunication:

- The groom sat beside his bride, family, and his annoying neighbor.
- The article featured the neighbors' uniquely-constructed house. It also featured their marriage and children.
- I have enclosed my photoshopped picture, my birth certificate, and a $40 check. (Notice I inserted additional words before the other two words to interrupt the "photoshopped" assumption.
- Enjoy your dorm, friends, and pre-approved business classes.
- The corporation's entrance has doormen and massive columns and statues.
- On her first day at work as an interior designer, Jayla's schedule included time set aside for her boss, filling out human resources forms, and her passion: color selection. (The original sentence could contribute to an even longer meeting with human resources!)

I hope these examples nudge you to re-read the lists you write and, if you need to, move words.

## 22. Four Words People Misuse:

We have all misused words. If you Google misused words, you'll find lists of them.

Here are four words I have personally heard misused—three said by authors I interviewed:

- PRODIGAL means being wastefully or recklessly extravagant; Being a spendthrift. It does not mean leaving home and living an immoral life—except for that spendthrift thing.

- AWESOME describes something that is magnificent, horrendous, or inspires overwhelming inspiration or fear—anything that causes us to drop our jaws in awe. God, the Northern Lights, a multi-car pile-up are awesome. However, most clothes, TV shows, songs, everyday comments, etc., are not awesome. Please take an additional second to think of the appropriate adjective. I thank you for that.

- PENULTIMATE means second to the last. It does not mean exceptional. This is my penultimate word.

- CONCERTED is used if two or more people take part. It means arranged or planned by agreement, It does not mean determined. One person cannot make a concerted effort. (con=with)

## 23. Here's a Word That's Almost Always Misused: "literally"

Is this correct or incorrect usage?

- Chris had us literally beside ourselves cracking up.
- That sunset literally blew my mind.
- She was literally a limp dish rag after that run.

(Answer: All three are incorrect.) In these cases, "literally" is a verbal filler. Some people may think it adds emphasis. It actually adds confusion. Did we clone ourselves and then break? Did our minds' blow? Did she turn into a limp dish rag?

Literally means actually; without exaggeration or inaccuracy. So, use the word only to emphasize the truth, not as verbal clutter that precedes an exaggeration. I love using the word when the situation embodies a cliché:

- Our German Shepherd's bark is literally worse than her bite. (Dinah is small for a German Shepherd, but she sounds as if she weighs 200 pounds. And she prefers licking to biting.)

Here is when the use of "literally" is appropriate:

- That two-year-old boy literally ran circles around his mother.
- Because the moss John planted stained his fingers, he finally could convince the garden club he literally has a green thumb.
- The miniature house in the museum was literally made of money.

When most people misuse "literally," they do so for emphasis or a verbal filler. Please don't be one of those people!

## 24. Common Usage Doesn't Mean It Always Makes Common Sense

Here are three words whose prefixes are unnecessary and irrational (Keep in mind the prefixes "un" and "ir" mean "not."):

- unthaw
- unloosen
- irregardless (Cringe. Yes, it has made it into the dictionary as nonstandard usage for regardless)

These words do not mean:

- unthaw — freeze
- unloosen – tighten
- irregardless – showing regard or concern for

"Regardless" means without regard, in spite of. "Irregardless" (not regardless) means the opposite.

Regardless of how many readers now know to avoid using these words, I feel anxious even typing the word "irregardless," which my computer dutifully underlined with a squiggly red line each time—and, in case you're wondering, no, I'm not going to "add it to my dictionary!"

## 25. How to Correctly Use "arguably"

This is, arguably, one of the most important tips of them all.

What did I just say? By using "arguably," I said this statement "is very possibly true even if it is not certainly true." (Merriam-Webster Dictionary) According to that dictionary, arguably could also mean:

- questionably
- susceptible to argument

Is that what we strive to say when we use this word?

("Arguably" also is an embedded suggestion to argue.)

When I hear people use it, most of the time, they either insert it as a verbal pause or filler word or they think it means "without a doubt."

Either way, they are misusing it, which is, arguably, a faux pas!

## 26. Is It a Podium or Lectern?

If you're making arrangements to give a speech, you will appreciate knowing the difference between these two words:

- If you request a podium, you will get a raised platform.
- If you request a lectern, you will get an elevated desk for your notes or laptop.

Podium comes from pod—foot. It's a place upon which we stand. (Think podiatrist or tripod.)

Lectern come from lect—to read. (Think lecture.)

Oh, and request a lavalier or headset mic. That way you can present without having to hold a microphone the whole time or be constrained by a mic attached to a lectern.

And you'll enjoy the experience even more!

## 27. Is It "lie" or "lay?"

The lie / lay conundrum.

Many Intelligent business leaders are foggy on this and think it's okay to say whatever they want. It's not.

Challenge: Learn the difference and start writing and saying the words correctly.

LIE: Use it If you, another person, or an animal reclines.

- Examples:
    - I love to lie in bed and read.
    - The cat prefers to lie next to her kittens.

Conjugating: lie / lay / lain:

- I lie on the beach.
- I lay on the beach all last week.
- I have lain so long I am sunburned.

LAY: Use it If you, another person, an animal, or an object is placed somewhere.

- Examples:
    - Lay the baby in the crib.
    - He will lay the book and the turtle next to the briefcase.
- Conjugating (This is easier!): lay / laid /laid:
    - Lay the proposal on the desk.
    - I laid it on the desk.
    - I have laid it on the desk.

You'll be glad when you lie down tonight to go to sleep that you also laid this previously confusing concept to rest!

## BEWARE OF TRENDY WORDS

### 28. Are You and Your Audience's Definitions Strikingly Opposite?

Is what you're saying good or bad?

For example:

- These hacks get results.
- She killed it in the meeting.

Hack: Are we talking about breaking into networks or—informal definition—making use of an efficient method for doing or managing something? (Dictionary.com)

Killed it: Did she do a phenomenal job or is she out a job? Did her presentation produce an irresistible effect or did she destroy the presentation? (Dictionary.com).

Before writing or speaking, consider your audience. You may have to give additional context, explain, or choose a more widely-understood word.

"A word to the wise is not sufficient if it doesn't make sense." (James Thurber, author and playwright)

## 29. Are You Inadvertently Confusing Your Audience?

Use caution with trendy adjectives that may mean the opposite of what you intend.

For example, in one month, I heard:

- We're going to have a ridiculously great church service today.
- That's an outrageous restaurant!

Remember that "ridiculous" comes from the verb "ridicule" and "outrageous" comes from "outrage."

I've also heard people loosely use "crazy" to represent wonderful and excellent. It's slang.

- His parents' mansion is crazy.
- That's crazy! (Habitual knee-jerk response)

Oh, and I'll add "insane."

- The meal was "insane." (delicious?)

Please remember the first definition for crazy, and all the definitions for insane pertain to mental illness. So, think what you might be communicating when you use these words, and if you are resorting to slang, delve a little deeper into your vocabulary to choose a more appropriate option.

# SECTION 4

# The Power of Words

"The word is a force; it is the power you have to express and communicate, to think, and thereby to create the events in your life...The word is so powerful that one word can change a life or destroy the lives of millions of people."

Don Miguel Ruiz, *The Four Agreements*

The right words, carefully chosen, can lift our spirits and the spirits of others. When we learn to use words wisely and well, we can harness that power and so much more.

In this section, we are going to explore the power of words. We are going to:

- Discover how words define us and how they can enhance our reputations.

- Focus on speaking positively and factually.

- Experience the joy, satisfaction, and rewards of asking good questions.

- Approach difficult conversations with resolutions and respect as the goals.

In this section, you'll increase your word power and learn skills to communicate better and connect positively.

Enjoy!

## WORDS DEFINE US

### 30. People Judge Us By Our Words

The Power of WORDS: The following is SUCCESS magazine's adaptation of "*The Jim Rohn Guide to Communication.*"

"People judge you by the words you use... Choose your words wisely... When you speak, use your words carefully.

- Avoid using words that will cause the other person to think poorly of you. Slang is one example. Another is, of course, slurs of any type.
- Use words that communicate positive values.
- <u>Use optimistic words,</u> words of strength. Make sure they are understandable.
- Use words that are colorful and rich with meaning, as long as the listener understands them."

The late Jim Rohn continues: "An expanded vocabulary will set you apart. It enhances the communication process and draws others in.

<u>Your vocabulary can reveal to others how educated you are,</u> and others may make judgments about you that can affect your opportunities with them. The best communicators will use an expanded vocabulary with more educated groups and a more basic vocabulary with less-educated groups."

Thank you, Jim Rohn and SUCCESS magazine, for championing the importance of words and exemplifying their impact.

## 31. "When in Rome, or in this case, London..."

Just when I thought I was asking the question perfectly, I learned I was confusing an entire culture!

While visiting England, I was fascinated by the differences in sentence structure.

Here's an example:

- In a restaurant, I asked, "Where are the restrooms?"
- That person replied, "You Americans talk as if you rest or bathe in those rooms." In England, the question is: "The toilet. Where is it?"

So, I started saying those words—in that order. Even though it felt awkward, I was amazed that people immediately understood.

It makes sense: It's a straight-forward request containing factual, essential information. We can learn a lot about how other cultures or countries prefer their phrases.

And on that trip, I noticed other countries embraced that word as well. In airports and train stations in Germany and Italy, versions of the word "toilet" graced signs on walls and doors.

So, I've learned to refrain from using our euphemistic "restroom" word in Germany, Italy, London—for starters. And all along, I thought I was "minding my manners."

## 32. Confidence-exuding Words

When speakers appear uncertain, their listeners remain unconvinced and struggle to connect.

To exude confidence, expunge confidence-robbing words such as "um, kinda, sorta, only, just, can't, you know, probably, like, afraid, I guess, I'll try, I mean."

Replace them with confidence-exuding words such as "I can, I will, I know, I am (reliable, confident, convinced), YES, absolutely!"

Change these sentences to confidence-exuding ones:

- I am just the assistant.
- You know, I mean, I'll try to get it done on time.
- I'm afraid we'll have to cancel our coffee meeting.
- Um, I kinda think this is important and sorta think you, like, might do it.

What confidence-robbing words or phrases are you habitually using that, starting right now, you're going to convert to confidence-exuding ones?

## SET THE STAGE FOR POSITIVITY

### 33. Embed Positive Commands

We have been embedding commands—positive and negative— all of our lives. We've told ourselves and others how to feel about and react to ideas, restaurants, movies, vacations, companies, people, etc.

We have said such comments as:

- You will enjoy that person (or class, etc.)
- You're going to meet Jerri? Be prepared to be bored with her stories!
- That project we're going to be working on will be difficult.
- I'm glad we'll have this challenge. I'm up for it!

We're going to focus on embedding positive commands, and the great news (which is an embedded positive command) is we can use them in our profession and life to intentionally program ourselves or others to accept, adjust to, and/or appreciate situations.

Some words and phrases to use when embedding commands are:

- Notice
- Love
- Like
- Realize
- Want
- Appreciate

- Be glad to
- Be pleased with
- Be happy about

Now here's a verbal challenge, which you'll find fascinating (another embedded positive command):

During this week, positively frame everything you say. This is a test of your verbal skills AND your attitude.

This means no gossiping or complaining. If you need to handle a negative situation, reframe your approach.

Examples:

- You'll appreciate that the project will be on your desk, mistake-proof, by Thursday. Instead of: I'm sorry, the project won't be done by Wednesday.
- I'll be glad to make the coffee. Instead of: Me make the coffee? Are you crazy?!
- My pleasure. Instead of: No problem.
- She's exhausted and has had a tough week. Instead of: She's such a _____!

Find an accountability partner who will also do this with you. You'll discover how much more effective and fun it will be. (You guessed it: yet another embedded positive command!)

## 34. Give Third-party Compliments

This practice is the opposite of gossiping about people. To make this a third-party compliment, we compliment the person or that person's attitude, effort, or achievements to another person—with that person being present.

When we speak positively of people in front of others: colleagues, friends, family members, people will grow into the conversations you have about them.

Also, engage in conversations that set expectations regarding that third person—expectations that:

- you know the person can achieve
- show you believe in him/her

This, according to business author John C. Maxwell who recommends you then personally follow up on these third-party compliments with reaffirming, empowering comments.

I suggest you take it a step further. On five different occasions this week, say something positive about five additional people without any of them being present. They may or may not ever know you said anything; however, their reputation—and yours will be enhanced.

What a positive, affirming way to add to your day!

## FACTS REIGN

### 35. Give Positive, Factual Compliments

Most people leave their jobs because they don't feel appreciated.

When complimenting someone, say more than, "Good job!" After a while, people realize that's a habitual throw-away phrase.

Enrich that phrase with WHY it's a good job. Add FACTS. And include the person's name. That makes the compliment even more personal.

Examples:

- John, you pulled off that event under budget and we had record attendance. Phenomenal Job! Thank you!

- Lisa, great work on the line today. You continue to produce over the quota. We appreciate you.

- Alex, I've come to depend on that smile of yours when you arrive every morning. You set the stage for the rest of us. Thank you.

- Thank you for picking up lunch again for us, Jay. We know you're as busy as we are, and we appreciate your taking time out of your schedule to do it.

The more a colleague or leader effectively compliments, the easier it is for employees to accept the occasional correctional feedback. That's because they know their boss appreciates them and, in the next day or two, they will hear yet another factual, positive compliment.

## 36. Choose Facts Over Opinions When Giving Feedback

When tactfully confronting a negative situation, lead with facts instead of opinions or emotions. According to the authors of *Crucial Conversations*, facts are the least controversial, the least insulting, and the most persuasive.

Example:

- Do not condescendingly approach the person with an opinion-laden statement such as:
  - "Because you couldn't get your lazy self out of bed this morning, the project we worked on blew up in our faces!"
- Instead, in a measured, respectful tone of voice, state the facts:
  - "Are you aware we needed you here at 7:30?" "We were to present our proposal at 8:00. You arrived at 8:25. At 8:10, Acme awarded the account to ON TIME, Inc. What happened?"
- Don't say:
  - "You did a lousy job on that proposal—and it's now officially late! What's wrong with you?"
- Instead say:
  - "You need to make some corrections in the proposal: check the date and the totals. Also, you need to use the latest, approved format. I'd like it on my desk in one hour. Can you make that happen? If you have any questions, I'm here."

# HARNESS THE POWER OF QUESTIONS

## 37. Ask Intriguing, Engaging Questions

The power of questions:

"It's not only the questions you ask but the questions you fail to ask that shape your destiny." That catalytic statement is from Author/Motivational Speaker Tony Robbins.

In her book, *The 7 Powers of Questions*, Dorothy Leed says questions are "the missing link to success."

She distilled her 20-years of research into these powerful results. She says questions:

1. Demand answers
2. Stimulate thinking
3. Give us valuable information
4. Put you in control
5. Get people to open up
6. Lead to quality listening
7. Get people to persuade themselves

To elaborate on the last point, people are more likely to believe what THEY realized than accept information fed by others. Dorothy Leed says, "[A] well-placed question can get their minds headed in a specific direction."

That's important information for people in authority and people questioning those in authority. Remember that the goal is to show respect.

For me, questions define and enrich my life and career; they always have! What are some of your favorite questions?

## 38. Ask Response-generating Questions When Hosting Virtual or Live Events

You and your audience want more substance from your guest. What sentences give you the best result?

You're the interviewer on a podcast, webinar, panel, TV show, or job interview and you want to make sure you are thorough in drawing out those you're interviewing. What do you say?

As a former TV reporter/anchor/host, I relied on these two sentences—and still find them indispensable:

- Tell me more.
    - This shows I'm listening, engaged, and honoring the person speaking.
- What else would you like to say?
    - I loved asking this question! The answers are fascinating and high energy: perfect sound bites!
    - Asking this question invites people to go in directions known only to them. Consequently, the conversations—or the TV stories—take intriguing twists!

What are your favorite response-generating sentences?

## 39. **The Best Question Ever!**

Transform this potentially-awkward conversation-starter question into the best question ever!

You're at an event—business or social—and you hear yourself ask, "What do you do?" You then suddenly hold your breath because what if the person says:

- I'm unemployed.
- I'm not working.
- I'm staying home with my children.
- Nothing. I'm retired.

The question sends the message that I assume the person is employed, which I, evidently, consider the preferred situation.

Instead of a conversation starter, that question sometimes becomes a conversation stopper. Have you ever tried to jump-start a conversation after it rolls backward into a ditch? It can be exhausting!

Here's the great news! A phenomenal alternative exists for "What do you do?". This alternative elicits enthusiasm, engagement, and respect. And, you will enjoy the other person's response because, regardless of where they are in their lives, their answers will be fascinating and energetic.

The best question ever is: "What are you working on?"

The authors of *Superconnector* recommend it in their book and say they learned it from author Vanessa VanEdwards.

I sometimes enhance the question and ask, "What are you working on that you're enjoying?" (or "that excites you?")

This question in its original form, or enhanced, promotes and encourages relationships, which is what connecting is all about!

## 40. Other Thought-generating Questions:

"What a great question!" When the person you're talking to says that, you know you've succeeded in fully engaging them.

Strive to come up with questions the other person will find fun, fascinating to answer, thought-provoking, and open-ended.

Here are some suggestions:

- What are you working on? (See the previous Communication Tip.)
- What's the most fascinating part/best part of your job?
- What have you learned or realized lately that has changed the way you think about something?
- What are you doing differently this year compared to last year?
- What do you tell people considering going into your field?
- Who do you admire most—and why?
- What was the best business decision you've ever made?
- What is one of the most catalytic or life-changing sentences you've ever uttered—besides saying, "Will you marry me?"
- What is your plan for 5 years from now?
- To what do you attribute your success?
- What advice do you—or would you—tell people just starting out in their careers that you wish someone had told you?
- How did you choose your career?

- What is one thing you do that surprises people when you tell them?

Obviously, the answers to these questions would fascinate me. What questions would you ask that would fascinate you?

Notice the answers to each of these intentionally open-ended questions require at least a sentence. The questions invite the person to think a little deeper, take inventory, examine, compare, and emotionally and energetically enjoy the process.

## 41. Questions to Avoid

We need to think before asking questions that cause others to question our confidence and intelligence.

Examples:

- Can you spell your name for me? (I would hope you can!) Instead say: Please spell your name.
- Can I ask a question? (You just did.)
- Can I interrupt? (Once again, you just did.)
- Can I talk to you? (Are you able to?) If so, how about saying one of the following:
  - Do you have a couple of moments to talk?
  - Is now a good time to talk to you?
  - May I talk to you for a few moments?

Here are questions to avoid when meeting someone or networking:

- How much money do you make?
- Are you divorced?
- How old are you?
- When is your baby due? (That one has backfired on even the savviest individuals!)

Depending on the circumstances, these questions raise doubts about our emotional intelligence and sense of propriety.

## 42. Be Fluent in Effective, Responsive Verbal Listening

Effective paraphrasing requires paying attention, summarizing the messages, and clarifying/validating feelings.

My recommendation: Create and continually update a list of adjectives describing positive and negative feelings. That way, you will be a prepared, fully-engaged listener.

Examples:

- You're relieved that the CEO approved the project, and I'm hearing some apprehension. Is that accurate?
- You said you feel belittled and ignored being constantly passed over for a promotion. That must be frustrating. I would struggle with that too.
- You're starting a business and already have 45 clients. How exciting! I'm impressed. What's your secret?

People appreciate being listened to. Paraphrasing and then tagging that paraphrase with a comment or a question honors them and their message.

Using the appropriate adjectives separates you from the person who thoughtlessly says, "So, things are going well at work. Cool!"

## MASTERING DIFFICULT CONVERSATIONS

### 43. Engaging the Other Person in Positive, Corrective Feedback

Here's a challenge: When giving corrective feedback, make it totally positive and engage the other person.

For example:

- What do you think went well during your presentation? What do you think you could have done even better? Let's talk about making that happen!

- I know you will appreciate this observation: When you talk with clients, instead of ending your phrases and statements with upward inflections ("up-talking"), how about if you speak with downward inflections? That way, you will sound more confident as you continue to look and be confident. What do you think about that?

Using positive, corrective, engaging feedback involves time-consuming, intentional composing—especially the first few times.

I recommend taking that time and putting in that effort. The results are win/win: Your employees correct the situations, AND they feel valued, encouraged, and empowered.

## 44. Corrective, Appreciation-driven Feedback

You will appreciate this!

That phrase is invaluable. When you use it, you tell other people how they are going to feel, and you compliment them on their ability to be discerning, to be teachable, and to truly appreciate what you are about to tell them.

If what follows is corrective feedback, you have communicated respect for them and the belief they will, indeed, appreciate the correction instead of feeling guilty or ashamed.

Which would you rather hear: "This might upset you..." or, "You're going to appreciate this..."

Remember: You are telling people how to feel and how you feel about them (an embedded positive command). Use that influence wisely. You and your team will appreciate it.

## 45. "Sticks and stones..."

Good morning, Stupid.

Now that I have elicited your attention (and your ire), convince me that words account for only a small percentage of communication.

In writing documents and emails, words — obviously — comprise most or all of the communication, even if one resorts to CAPITALIZING or emoticons ☺.

Let's get back to speaking: If someone says, "Good morning, Stupid" in an affectionate embrace using a tender tone of voice, those loving non-verbals still don't eclipse the innately insulting "Stupid." We cannot dismiss "Stupid" as being a measly 7% or 8% of an otherwise affirming communication.

Here is another example where words eclipse tone of voice and body language:

- Alex's boss invites him into her office and diplomatically and professionally says, "You're fired."
- Alex leaves her office — not reflecting on how respectful and professional she is.
- He leaves stunned because his world just collapsed.
- Why? Two words: "You're fired."

Words are powerful. So are a person's tone of voice and body language. We've all experienced the incongruence of the message when the three don't align. Just think of the effects of name-calling bullies or sarcastic "friends."

Be circumspect in the words you use and how you deliver them. And if the message is a tough one for others to hear, do your best to deliver it clearly, empathetically, and respectfully.

## 46. Respectfully Confronting Crucial Conversations

"People never become defensive about what you're saying. They become defensive because of why they think you're saying it." (Joseph Grenny, co-author of *Crucial Conversations*)

When embarking on those crucial conversations, think about your desired outcome. Grenny says to show mutual respect, start with defining your mutual purpose, so the person realizes you care about his/her interests, problems, and concerns.

According to the authors of *Crucial Conversations*, "The instant people perceive disrespect in a conversation, the interaction is no longer about the original purpose—it is now about defending dignity... They resort to pouting, name-calling, yelling, and making threats."

The authors advocate stopping, re-focusing, immediately addressing the perceived situation, and restoring it by showing mutual respect and defining mutual purpose.

Emphasize intent over content.

I'll add: To make sure you communicate your desired intent, think about how your comments MIGHT come across and adjust your words, tone of voice, and expression, so they align with how you WANT your message to be received.

Often, after I've established mutual respect, if I need to address a crucial conversation, I use the phrase, "Are you aware...?" It's non-threatening because you are asking about their awareness— not cornering them into an uncomfortable situation. In that non-threatening manner, the other person also receives the respectful, intended message.

Sometimes, I start with, "You'll appreciate this, are you aware...?" In doing that, I'm also telling them how I'm expecting them to respond (appreciatively).

It works!

# SECTION 5

# Words to Omit or Avoid

"Omit needless words" is the mantra of professional writing. Nearly every student of writing hears this phrase from a teacher or reads it in a book on writing.

And it especially applies in business. Can you imagine having to wade through legal, medical, technical, or financial documents that contain verbal fillers, redundancies, or ambiguous writing? Some of us can do more than imagine, we have experienced it!

To sharpen your verbal edge, you'll need to pare down the fillers. In this section, we identify and eliminate verbal clutter and other phrases or words that keep us from being succinct.

Honing the skill of self-editing improves with practice, and the results are worth the scrutiny: excellent writing; articulate presenting; and engaged readers and audiences.

Also, in this section, you'll learn how to make your messages perfectly clear for your readers and listeners.

We will start by clarifying and supercharging your writing. To do that, we'll eliminate one phrase.

# SAY IT DIFFERENTLY – YOU'LL LIKE THE RESULTS

## 47. Eliminate "there is, are, was, etc."

Do you want to instantly become a noticeably better speaker or writer?

By eliminating two words, you create active, succinct sentences.

The words? there is, there are, there were

Example:

- Avoid saying: "There is a dog that barks."
- Say instead: "A dog barks."

Notice the subject (dog) and verb (barks) now take control of the sentence and demand attention.

More examples of eliminating "there:"

- Avoid saying: She knows there were better alternatives.
- Say instead: She knows better alternatives existed.

- Avoid saying: There will be a concert on May 12.
- Say instead: The concert is on May 12.

- Avoid saying: There had been hints they chose to ignore for years.
- Say instead: They chose to ignore the hints for years.

- Avoid saying: There are more examples I could give you.
- Say instead: I could give you more examples.

## 48. **Give "it" a Rest. Choose Active Voice**

Do you involve "it" in too many sentences?

- Instead of saying, "It has come to my attention..."
- Say, "I have learned...".

- Instead of saying, "It is recommended..."
- Say, "I recommend...", "The board recommends..."

- Instead of saying, "It is a pleasure working with you".
- Say, "I enjoy working with you."

- Instead of saying, "It has to be settled."
- Say, "We need to settle this."

In the above examples, we changed the subject and verb from 'it is" to words that have precise meaning and action—we moved from passive to active voice.

> So, instead of saying, "It is the active voice that makes your ideas clear and strong."
>
> Say, "Active voice makes your ideas clear and strong."

## 49. Are You Having "Guy" Trouble?

When speaking professionally to groups, refrain from saying "guys." If you eliminate that word, you will sound more professional.

The first meaning of "guy" is "a man or a boy: fellow." Its second meaning is: "informal: persons of either sex: people." (Dictionary. com). The British Dictionary doesn't include the second meaning.

I hear, "you guys," from professional speakers, church leaders and staffs, and executives giving presentations.

When I started teaching English, I was surprised to hear myself saying, "Okay, guys, I need your attention." I worked to eliminate it immediately. It took a few days.

That's because the reward—for the listeners—is immeasurably greater:

- Instead of saying, "Good morning, guys. Are you guys ready for...?"
- You say: "Good morning. Are you ready for...?"

We relate personally and less like, well, coaches talking to their teams of all men.

And if you're still thinking of using "guys," think of the second meaning: "Informal: persons of either sex: people."

- "Good morning, people. Are you people ready...?"

Do you really want to communicate that way?

## 50. Get This: Sometimes You Need to Avoid "get" or "got"

Think before using GET or GOT.

The correct word might be HAVE, HAS or HAD. In fact, most of the time, that's the case!

- Avoid saying: "I got to go now."
- Say instead: "I have to go now."

- Avoid saying: "Do you GOT your gloves?"
- Say instead: "Do you HAVE your gloves?"

Also, using HAVE or HAS as helping words doesn't dignify the faux pas.

- Avoid saying: "He's got three sisters." (The "he's" means he has, so you're saying, "He has got three sisters.)
- Say instead: "He has three sisters."

Here is an appropriate use of "get": "Please get the shoes on the topic shelf."

Do you HAVE the concept?

## AVOID! AVOID! AVOID!

### 51. Verbal Clutter: Saboteurs of Our Messages

Expunge your verbal clutter.

I mean, the fact of the matter is, it's probably kinda one of those pretty cool things where you, basically, really really need to do this each and every time. To be real honest with you, that being said, you just actually should! It's, like, awesome! Do you know what I mean? That's the bottom line, I'm just saying. Um...whatever.

What did the writer/speaker say?

- Almost nothing! And if a morsel did exist, the verbal clutter eclipsed and devoured it.

What did the writer/speaker demonstrate?

- Lack of preparation and focus
- Lack of self-respect and respect for the listeners and their time
- A disregard for succinctness and concise vocabulary
- The need to be the center of attention at any cost—and fulfilling that need by being relentlessly loquacious--content or no content
- Lack of discipline in expunging verbal clutter
- Possible lack of knowledge of what to expunge
- (Insert your additional assessments here!)

To avoid this verbal avalanche of filler words, have well-thought-out and well-practiced comments ready — even if the comment is, "I want to think about that. I'll give you a response in a couple of minutes."

## 52. **Verbal Clutter During a TV Interview**

"The only thing worse than saying nothing is spending a long time saying it." (*Toastmasters* magazine)

Preparation for speeches, networking, sales presentations, and TV interviewing is key—even if you have only seconds to prepare.

I watched as a TV host interviewed a professional couple. The host directed the first question to the woman. Her response and delivery conveyed knowledge and confidence. The next question went to the man. His first words were, "Um, I guess, you know...I mean...kinda..."

The man was just as familiar with the topic as the woman; however, he obviously hadn't thought ahead of time about what he would say. So, he chose to think about his response as he uttered a long sentence of filler words.

If he had prepared, he would have launched into the answer, eliminated the verbal clutter, and immediately engaged the listeners. Instead, he rambled, tuned out his listeners, communicated insecurity, and sabotaged his credibility and message.

## 53. Examples of Verbal Clutter: Be Afraid. Be Very Afraid!

Strive to eliminate these words and phrases:

- um, ah, uh
- like
- you know
- I mean
- sort of, kind a
- just, only
- pretty much
- by and large
- what not
- what have you

- basically
- goes without saying
- be that as it may
- interestingly enough
- It has been brought to my attention that...
- for all intents and purposes...
- needless to say
- the fact of the matter is...
- It's one of those things where you...
- that being said

- honestly, frankly
  - Never say this. It draws attention to the fact that you've been lying up to now and will continue to lie after you've finished this sentence.
- to be perfectly honest/candid with you...
  - This is an even longer phrase that says the same as the previous words.
  - What you might be wanting to say is: "I'm going to be transparent here..."
- I just want to write and say...
  - Drop this needless phrase and immediately say or write what you want to say.
- without further ado

–   Ado means confusion or messing around.

–   When you introduce the presenter and tell the audience why they should care about the content, does it make sense to say, "Without confusing you further, here's Dr. Chris Stevens."  Or, "We're done messing around. Here's Dr. Chris Stevens."

–   Say instead:

> "Let's welcome...."  or "Ladies and gentlemen, Dr. Chris Stevens."

## 54. Verbal Disclaimers: ("I don't mean to be critical, but...")

When someone starts a comment with "I don't mean to be critical..." What do we do? We brace ourselves to be criticized.

These introductory comments are called verbal disclaimers. In my opinion, they are called "disclaimers" for the benefit of the people saying them--not for the people hearing them. In other words, the person delivering the message thinks, *I'm giving them a disclaimer, if that they choose to take offense, it's their problem!*

These foreboding spoiler alerts—disclaimers—are ostensibly said out of sincere concern for others. However, the opposite occurs: The disclaimers' messages hit us deeper than we realize. We hear "I don't mean to be critical but..." and we actually hear, "I mean to be critical." That's because our subconscious minds struggle with processing the words "no" and "not."

Here are some other verbal disclaimers:

- Don't take this personally...
- I mean no disrespect...
- I don't mean to be rude...
- I'm not saying you're acting inappropriately...
- I don't mean to interrupt...

The remedy? If you're tempted to deliver something negative as a disclaimer, think before you speak, eliminate that opening comment, and proceed respectfully.

What other verbal disclaimers immediately warn us to be on guard?

## 55. Redundancies

Reduce verbal clutter by eliminating redundancies.

Here are some examples of redundancies. Whatever is in the parenthesis is not needed:

| | | |
|---|---|---|
| (added) bonus | (advanced) planning | gather (together) |
| (honest) truth | (unpaid) volunteer | kneel (down) |
| (close) proximity | collaborate (together) | revert (back) |
| every (single) | eradicate (completely) | report (back) |
| consensus (of opinion) | follow (after) | postpone (until later) |
| (mutual) cooperation | PIN (number) | (sum) total |
| surrounded (on all sides) | (temper) tantrum | tall (in stature) |
| (usual) custom | visible (to the eye) | nodded (his head) |

Many more redundancies exist.

What verbal clutter redundancies drive you crazy?

# OMIT THE SLANG WORDS FOR "SAID"

### 56. Just Say "said."

The words "like" and "go, goes, went" have become ubiquitous slang for "said:"

Example:

- I was like, "You won't believe this!" And he goes, "Try me!" So, I went, "Okay!"

Regardless of the popularity, it's not professional-speak, and your listeners are aware of that.

Imagine a news anchor saying (notice I didn't say "going"), "The suspect was like, "I'm not guilty!"

One of my news directors told us to always use "said" when introducing quotes and soundbites. And he didn't care how many times in a story we used it.

"Said" is an objective verb. ("Asked" works if the person quoted asked a question.) Unfortunately, I am now also hearing and reading "claimed" in the newspapers and nightly news, and, as a former TV reporter/anchor, I'm stunned it gets past the editors. "Claims" shows the reporter or anchor's opinion about the veracity of the person's quote or remark. And reporter's opinions have no place in objective journalism.

Start today to eliminate "like, go, goes, and went" as lead-ins to what people said.

Think of "said" as your default lead-in. And if you need more options, here are some other objective words:

- asked
- added
- proposed
- acknowledged
- testified
- questioned
- recommended
- announced
- stated

## 57. Beware of Saying, "I says."
## (Yes, some people are saying this!)

"I says." (Who says that?!)

You would be shocked at how "I says" is insidiously inserting itself into the phrases that introduce dialogue.

And, incredibly, those who say this seem blissfully unaware of their grammatical faux pas. It's a problem on two levels:

- It's oh-so grammatically incorrect—we need to say, "I say."
- It's used in the wrong tense. When we quote ourselves or others, it's usually in the past tense. So, we need to say, "I said." If it's present tense, say, "I say."

Here is how this misuse evolved:

In recounting a conversation, a person may say: "John says... and then I says... and then Alex says...."

Even though the conversation may have occurred last week, the person recounting it talks as if it is ongoing—in the present tense. So, instead of saying "John said" and "I said," the person says, "John says."

These may be the same people who also say, "John was like... and then I go...and then Mary went...."

Please, just say "said."

Here are some more examples of misusing "says":

- I saw Zach last night and he says he was tired.
- Yesterday, she says she went to the doctor.

- I heard their short conversation. Jean says, "No, I won't go." Then Randi says, "Why not?"

If you know anyone who has started to say this, and who would appreciate your respectfully bringing it to their attention, please do so.

# SECTION 6

# Change Negatives to Positives

You're going to love this section! We're going to turn the negative phrases we've been conditioned to use—and don't even realize it—into powerful words of positivity.

You'll appreciate the words, phrases, and sentences you can choose to use instead of the negative ones you'll be discarding. And those with whom you interact will detect the difference.

Let's start making that change now!

## SIGNS OF BEING PRONE TO NEGATIVITY

### 58. Engrained NegativeSpeak:

We sometimes speak negatively without realizing it. We say such things as:

- I'm afraid I'll have to work overtime. (Really? Afraid?)
- It wouldn't hurt to give him a call. (Again...really?)
- I hate to tell you your team lost last night. (What else do you hate to say?)
- We couldn't ask for better friends. (Why not?)
- That's awfully nice. (Is that a bad nice?)
- I can't complain. (Oh, yes you can!)

You'll be amazed at what you are actually saying!

## 59. Pessimists vs. Optimists

Are you broadcasting negative self-fulfilling prophesies?

Here are two negative examples:

- I knew this would happen: Every time I'm on a team, something goes wrong.
- You're not catching any fish because I'm in your boat. This happens all the time.
- I have the worst shopping line Karma. Whatever line I chose at the checkout, it will always be the slowest.
- Just my luck. (This never implies good luck)

For pessimists, one negative incident can pervade all other experiences.

For optimists, the negative incident is an isolated situation from which optimists learns and get on with their lives.

If you work with a pessimist, encourage that person and diplomatically and respectfully counter that person's comments with facts to the contrary. And add a compliment, if applicable.

Pessimists can change their perspectives. Be optimistic about that!

# EVEN POSITIVE PEOPLE SPEAK NEGATIVELY — AND THEY DON'T KNOW IT!

## 60. Negative Phrases: Why We Inadvertently Use Them

"I'll see if I can't get that information to you today."

(Why would I say that I'll see if I CANNOT get that information for you?)

Maybe we say this because we trust that phrase to deliver its message and we haven't stopped to scrutinize what we—and others—are saying.

Today, let's see if we CAN rid our sentences of the negative words that derail our communication.

For several examples of phrases laced with unintended negatives, check out my article "You Don't Say!" on www.TheVerbalEdge.com.

## WHY CHANGE NEGATIVES TO POSITIVES

### 61. Negative Phrases Cause Unintended Results

I dropped off a document for my husband at his office and thanked the receptionist for giving it to him. She said, "No worries."

I was taken aback because I had not thought to worry.

This is an example of a negative embedded command, much the same as if the receptionist would have said, "No problem." (I didn't think it would be a problem. Evidently, she considered the possibility! Now, I'm wondering if she's giving me a clue. This is, indeed, embedded!)

Remember, our minds skip over the words NO, NOT and N'T (What if I told you, "Do not think of a green squirrel?" You have to first think of one before wiping out the image. The same goes for thinking about worries and problem.)

Instead, respond positively: "My pleasure / I'm happy to do that / Any time / You are welcome, etc."

## 62. **Negative Phrases Are Confusing**

"This is not a subject with which I am not familiar."

Yes, I heard someone say this, and I stared in disbelief!

Think quickly: What did that person mean? (Translation: "I'm familiar with this subject.")

See how confusing and unproductive negative words inserted into phrases/sentences can be!

Ready for some examples? Here goes:

- Don't arrive after 3:00. (Arrive by 3:00.)

- Why don't I stop by and pick it up? (How about if I stop by...)

- He mentioned it no less than 10 times. (He mentioned it at least...)

- It will not take a minute for you to read this. (So, how long will it take?)

- They did not lack for opportunity. (They had plenty of opportunities ...)

- We can't agree. (We see things differently.)

- I'll see if I can't do that for you. (Literal meaning: "I'll try not to be able to do that! Intended meaning: "I'll see if I CAN do that...)

- They will stop at nothing to do that. (They will persevere / keep at it, etc....)

- No problem: a response to "Thank You." ("My pleasure.") I'm usually tempted to say, "I hope it isn't a problem. I wouldn't want to cause a problem."

- Not to mention... (We all know how this ends: The person immediately mentions it!)

## 63. More Confusing, Negatively-constructed Phrases

These phrases all contain "DON'T, NOT, or N'T.

More confusing negative phrases, we don't realize we say:

- Wouldn't you agree?
- You don't have public restrooms, do you" (I heard that while on vacation.)
- More times than not...
- Don't spill that glass of milk. (The glass is on the edge of the table.)
- You won't be disappointed.
- Don't forget to... (Our subconscious minds skip over "don't" and "not", so we hear "forget to...")

Say instead:

- Do you agree?
- Do you have public restrooms?
- Usually
- Move that glass closer to the center of the table.
- You'll be fascinated/be glad you did, etc.
- Remember to...

## 64. Negative Phrases Can Backfire

Here are some negatively-constructed sentences that sabotage the messages:

- Enjoy this and, in no uncertain circumstances, don't refrain from using.

- I'll see if I can't get that done.

- Don't take this the wrong way...

- You don't understand me. (Hint: start this changed sentence with "I...")

- That's not a half-bad restaurant and it's not far from here.

- Unfortunately, right now, we don't have that in stock.

- You are nothing if not conscientious.

- Am I catching you at a bad time?

- I'm out of the office and won't be back until Monday.

- You are not wrong.

- I'll see if I can't get that done.

- It's not atypical to experience that.

How would you change these sentences to make them more receiver friendly?

I'll start you with the first sentence and when you're finished with all of them, look below for some suggestions:

- Enjoy this and keep using it. (See how different it feels?)

---

- I'll see if I can get that done.

- (Say nothing. Proceed with the thought and do it

respectfully.)

- I'm struggling to understand. Could you please explain this?

- That's a good restaurant and it's near here.

- You'll be glad to know we will have that in stock in a week, and then we'll send it right to you.

- You are extremely conscientious.

- Am I catching you at a good time?

- I'm out of the office and will be back on Monday.

- You are correct.

- I'll see if I can get that done.

- It's typical to experience that.

(What I don't do for you!)

## 65. "Thank You" Deserves Positive Responses

Ubiquitous negative or knee-jerk responses to "thank you" warrant another reminder for all of us.

When responding to "Thank you," please SMILE and say something positive, such as:

- My pleasure.
- Glad to do it.
- Any time.
- You're welcome.

Avoid, "No problem." (You're saying it could be a problem, but you've decided, in this case, it isn't.)

Also refrain from saying: yup, yep, yeah, or uh huh.

Think content. Refrain from responding automatically: I watched as a TV meteorologist responded to "Thank you" with "You bet." What does that mean?

A positive, intentional response to "Thank you" communicates you are a positive, intentional person.

# Networking

At some point, if you're in business, whether as the CEO of your own company or as an employee, you will most likely be tasked to attend one or more networking meetings or events.

Networking happens when and where you take the initiative to meet someone, ask about their interests and business and share information about your interests and business. Networking also takes place when you respond to the other person initiating a conversation with you.

Networking occurs at conferences, conventions, or events specifically for networking. It also occurs in grocery lines, ticket lines, bathroom lines, Bible studies, concerts, coffee shops, backyards, parties—anywhere two or more people reach out to one another. The intent is relationship building, possibly collaborating, and maybe eventually entering into a business relationship.

In that instance and in networking events where people take turns introducing themselves, you might include a 30-second or a 1-minute well-constructed description of your businesses, service, clients, etc. Many people call these elevator speeches or commercials—pitches you deliver in the time it takes to ride with someone for a few floors in an elevator. (I had that experience with the Mayor of St. Petersburg, Florida!)

This section is dedicated to helping you to professionally prepare for these situations. You'll learn the foundational aspects that will strengthen your preparation, your approach, and your credibility. What you say may change with every fascinating encounter, and the more confident and relationship-focused you become, the more successful you will be.

# GETTING MENTALLY PREPARED

## 66. Networking: It's All in Your Head!

Before approaching others: think and define.

- Think how you'll enjoy meeting others and learning from them.

- Think how much they will enjoy meeting and learning from you.

- Define who you are or who you want to be (bold, engaged, creative, etc.)

- Affirm yourself several times before you arrive. For example, think:

  - I am confident, engaging, interested in others, and interesting. People enjoy me and are glad we connect.

- Be prepared with insightful and engaging questions. For examples and ideas, review Harnessing the Power of Questions in the "Power of Words" section in this book: Tips #37-42.

After you've done practiced your affirmation a few times a day, you'll embody that confident and interesting person who enjoys networking with colleagues, clients, family members, neighbors, and friends.

That's congruity, and according to *The Charge* author Brenden Burchard, when our actions are congruent, we feel more grounded, responsible and self-assured.

I further define the results as integrity.

We can change our trajectory by doing and believing something new and sticking with it. We all have the options to become who we want to be.

## MEETING OTHERS AND GETTING THEIR NAMES RIGHT

### 67. Forgot Their Name? Retrieve It Easily and Painlessly, Part 1

We all encounter this embarrassing situation: We recognize people but are unable to recall their names.

Here is a solution that works nearly every time.

- While shaking their hands, say, "Good to see you. To remind you, I'm ..." and then say your first and last name.

- Usually, the other person or people will reciprocate with their names.

I use this technique frequently. And people I've met have mercifully introduced themselves again for me.

Sometimes, I had remembered their names and told them so. Other times, I thanked them for reminding me. Every time, I've been impressed with their intuitiveness and relationship skills.

If people don't say their names when you're mentioning your name, then smile and casually say, "Remind me of your name." (And then incorporate their name into your conversation a few times.) "Remind me of your name" is quick, easy, and almost unnoticeable.

And it's more professional and less traumatic than making a big deal out of forgetting their names and launching into how embarrassed you are.

Or worse: proclaiming you're not good at remembering names, which is an excuse and automatically puts the other people into the category of "not worth remembering." And they know it.

Decide the people you meet ARE worth knowing. You can do it. Pretend you have a teenage daughter and you're meeting her new boyfriend. You would not only remember his name; you would google it as soon as he left!

More on this on the next page.

## 68. Forgot Their Name? Retrieve It Easily and Painlessly, Part 2

More ways to retrieve names that escape us:

You're at an event, and you see people you think you've met before. If you're with your spouse or someone who also knows these people, use this game plan:

> Beforehand, agree to casually mention the first and last names of people you encounter.
>
> For example, your companion can say "You remember Dave and Sally Harris." To which you can happily say, "Sure!"
>
> That's because you did remember them—just not their names. Your companion can also add how you know these people. (Extra points!)

Here's another tactic—recommended by Heather McMichael, a friend and former TV broadcasting colleague.

> She says, "If I'm with my husband, and I recognize a face but not a name I will introduce my [husband] and then the other person will always say their name."

I've almost always had success with that, too. However, I've also encountered people who just say, "Hello." So, I then resort to my favorite, simple request: "Remind me of your name."

## INTRODUCING YOURSELF TO A GROUP:

### 69. Effectively Saying Your Name, Company, and Elevator Speech

You're at a networking event, and it's your turn to stand up and introduce yourself to the group. YIKES!

Here is one way to get and keep your prospects' attention:

- Stand tall, smile, and then confidently, clearly (pause between key words), and energetically tell the group your first and _last_ name, your title, and the name of your company.

- Then say, "I help (name the target group), state the results those prospects will experience, and how they will feel about those results.)"

- Then repeat your name and your company's name because NOW the people at the event are suddenly interested.

Here's one way I introduce myself at networking events:

"I'm Elizabeth MacDonald. I'm a communication skills advisor. My company is The Verbal Edge.

I help teams and individuals who value communication skills excel in presenting themselves and their messages, so they can feel confident when speaking, writing emails, and engaging others."

If you have a full minute, you can give examples of the pain some of your clients experienced before using your products or services:

"My clients typically want to polish their communication skills: some are nervous about talking in public, some are embarrassed because they aren't sure about their grammar skills, and still others avoid approaching and correcting aggressive people for fear of being bullied or yelled at. If you or anyone you know has these problems, talk to me after the meeting. I'm Elizabeth MacDonald, The Verbal Edge." (I learned this approach by attending Sandler Sales Training.)

Do you want people to pay attention to your elevator speech, to care, and to become clients? If so, take time to select your words, prepare—so you'll look and feel confident, smile, connect with the group, and deliver knowing you have this!

## ENDING CONVERSATIONS AND MERGING OUT

### 70. Interrupt Yourself!

Yes, you read it correctly. Interrupt yourself! It's the secret to merging out gracefully, professionally, and respectfully.

For a minute, so you can put yourself in this situation, pretend you're the other person and you have just finished answering a question. As soon as you say the last word, the person who asked you the question says, "I need to go now. Nice talking to you."

How do you feel? Are you thinking, "Obviously that person could hardly wait for me to stop talking and wasn't listening at all!

The way to remedy that is to be the last person talking and then when you've finished, mention you need to leave.

That way, instead of interrupting the other person's flow, you've done it to yourself, and you can smoothly transition out of the conversation.

(The next tip will have more on how to do that.)

## 71. Making Good Lasting Impressions:

When engaging in a networking conversation, the last impression you make needs to be as good as your first impression.

We've all experienced this: You want to end a conversation and talk to someone else. Here is a professional and positive way do that: "I enjoyed catching up with you/meeting you and especially appreciate learning about _____. I look forward to connecting with you again."

Mike Bechtle, author of *Confident Conversations,* says we need to end conversations the way we began them:

- Smile.
- Give warm, firm handshakes.
- Use the names of the people to whom you were speaking.
- Tell them how much we:
    - appreciate meeting them.
    - value them.
    - learned about the topics you discussed.

Summarizing a point the other person made honors that person and shows you were laser-focused and found the information valuable.

This is also the time to ask if you could exchange business cards. Remember to look at the other person's card for a couple of seconds and possibly make a comment. That shows you respect the person and what he/she does.

Oh, and when you give your card to someone else, when that person takes it, hold on to it for a split second to communicate the importance you place on it.

For the past two years, I've been doing that and taking time to look at and appreciate the other person's card before putting it in my purse or pocket. What a difference that makes!

# Grammar – Learn to love it

You saw this coming: grammar DOs and DON'TS.

If you're like me, you want to know you're presenting your words—and by extension, your message—precisely, accurately, clearly—devoid of any distractions and confusion caused by the wrong punctuation, tense used, word, or location in a sentence.

We've all made these mistakes, and we've all learned from them.

These tips will remind you of some rules and enlighten you of others.

I hope you enjoy the selection of tips I've chosen—grammar faux pas I've seen CEOs make and grammar mistakes that are rampant and, most of the time, undetected or dismissed.

Be that person whose writing reflects your wisdom and integrity in every way—right down to your use of gerunds, apostrophes, hyphens, and capitalization.

Absorb these 101 communication skills tips, including these grammar rules...and rule the world! Okay, I overstated that.

Take two: Absorb these 101 communication skills tips including these grammar rules...and confidently influence the world.

Yes!

## WHICH IS CORRECT?

### 72. Your vs. You're

Is it "your" or "you're?"

This is one of the most common challenges writers face. (The words in the next two tips are also members of that club!)

Simply put:

- "You're" means "you are." "Your" does not.
- "Your" is possessive. Period. Examples: Your cat. Your career.

More examples of both words:

- Your use of the words you're writing indicates you're starting to master this.
- You're the composer of your thoughts and messages.

Oh, and don't trust your spell check. Many times, my spell check erroneously prompts me to change "you're" to "your."

Test your choice: When in doubt, write out "you are" instead of "you're." (It's more professional, too.)

## 73. It's vs. Its

Refrain from doing what you might automatically want to do! That's what I had to teach myself.

Years ago, I, like many people, thought that "its" was ALWAYS written it's. My reasoning was simple. It is either a:

- contraction for "it is" and contractions always substitute an apostrophe for one or more missing letters.
- Possessive. And possessives have apostrophes.

I WAS WRONG, WRONG, WRONG!

Yes, we use the apostrophe for the contraction it's, which means "it is."

However, NO *possessive* pronoun or *possessive* adjective contains an apostrophe! NOT ONE! And we are talking *possessive*!

<u>Look and be amazed</u>:

| Possessive Pronouns | Possessive Adjectives | Contractions: |
|---|---|---|
| my | mine | I'm |
| your | yours | you're |
| his | his | he's |
| her | hers | she's |
| ITS | ITS | IT'S |
| our | ours | we're |
| their | theirs | they're |

So, when you realize it is possessive, resist the temptation to add an apostrophe.

It's a way to stop its confusion.

## 74. **To vs. Too**

Are you writing "to" when you mean "too"?

I see this mistake frequently—even in emails from people who are, otherwise, excellent writers.

"Too," the longer of the two words, has the longer list of meanings: extremely, more than desirable, also, very, or indeed.

"To" is a preposition: it connects.

Examples:

- People may be too hurried or too distracted to focus on these words.
- These two misspellings are too frequent and may be the result of being too indifferent to the difference.
- They could be too confident, too.

Here's to learning!

## 75. I or Me? When in Doubt...

When in doubt, leave the other word out.

That's my mantra when teaching individual clients and workshop attendees whether to use "I, she, he" (subject pronouns) or "me, her, him" (object pronouns).

Examples:

- John and me went to the meeting. (Test it: Leave out John: "Me went to the meeting." That's wrong.)
- Correct: "John and I went to the meeting."

- This is the email her and I sent. (Test it: "This is the email her sent.")
- Correct: "This is the email she and I sent."

- The VPs praised Chris and I. (Test it: "The VPs praised I.")
- Correct: "The VPs praised Chris and me."

Another clue: You never combine the pronouns "him" or "her" with "I". And you never use "she" or "he" with "me."

Example:

- Him and me completed the project. (Test it: "Him completed the project. Me completed the project.")
- Correct: "He and I completed the project."

## 76. **We or Us**

Is it "we" or "us?"

- We writers need to know the better choice for us wordsmiths.
- We, the people, ...

The rule is simple: Pretend the word *after* "us" or "we" is not there and choose what sounds better.

- We [*] need to know the better choice for us [*].

More examples:

- We neighbors are concerned.
- He will be speaking to us employees.
- The candidate met with us constituents to see if we voters were satisfied.

For us professionals, knowing this rule means we can write and speak with even more confidence.

## 77. **Which vs. That**

Which vs. That.

Use "which" to describe nonessential information—set apart by commas.

- The phone, which Dan never liked, fell into the hot soup.
- The XYZ Project, which took months to complete, won an award.

Use "that" to describe essential information.

- Dan scooped out the phone that fell into the hot soup.
- The project that won the award took months to complete.

Bonus:

Use "who" for people:

- The CEO who endorsed the project denounced it. In this case, it's essential to know the CEO endorsed the project, so that information is NOT enclosed by commas.

## 78. **Well vs. Good**

De-murking the WELL/GOOD conundrum: When do we use WELL and GOOD?

WELL is an adverb. It modifies verbs and answers the question How: He slept well, ran well, spoke well, worked well.

GOOD is an adjective. It modifies nouns and answers the question WHAT (kind/type): He had a good time, good run, good speech and she did a good job. Usually when you use "good," the noun it modifies follows it.

And sometimes that noun precedes it:

- This example is good.

Now, to introduce a little murk: the exception. When linking verbs are involved, both WELL and GOOD can be used. "A linking verb connects [links] the subject with a word that gives information about the subject's condition or a relationship." * (Some linking verbs are is, are, was, were, am, be, appear, look, feel, seems, sound, taste)

- I am well.
- I am good.
- I sound/appear/look/feel good.
- I sound/appear/look/feel well.

If someone asks about a person's health, the better answer is, "I am well." If someone asks how they're doing in general or if they are okay, a person could say, "I'm good."

So, heed well this good advice!

*YourDictionary.com

# 79. **Went vs. Gone**

"I would have went to the meeting." Are you cringing?

The sentence needs to say, "I would have GONE to the meeting."

Here is how we conjugate this verb:

| Subject | Present | Past | Present perfect |
|---|---|---|---|
| I | go | went | have/had **gone** |
| You | go | went | have/had **gone** |
| He/she/it/Ella | goes | went | has/had **gone** |
| we | go | went | have/had **gone** |
| they | go | went | have/had **gone** |

Conjugating this verb may seem elementary; however, you would be amazed at how many people have gone out of their way to ask that I create this tip and post it!

That's because the misuse of this one verb is widespread. Entire regions of the United States say this incorrectly and many otherwise well-spoken people are unaware that "gone" is used in the present perfect tense and beyond.

Since I, too, cringe when I hear "would have went," I enthusiastically hope this tip will make "would have went" a goner!

## PLEASE CAPITALIZE!

### 80. Capitalize the First Word in Sentences and All Proper Nouns.

Capitalize the first word of every sentence. No exceptions.

Refrain from starting those sentences with numbers:

- The year 2017 was life-changing for the Johnson family.

Capitalize:

- Proper nouns: specific persons, places, or things.
- Proper nouns used as descriptors of food, animals, and other items:
  - She loves English muffins, Danish rolls, Swedish meatballs, and Canadian bacon.
  - The audience watched as the German shepherd played Chinese checkers.
  - English muffins
  - Danish rolls
  - Swedish meatballs
  - Canadian bacon
  - Hungarian goulash
  - doubting Thomas
  - Chinese checkers
  - Simon says

- German shepherd
- even Steven
- Jack of all trades

## 81. Capitalize Names and Words Used Instead of Them.

Capitalize:

- Names
- Words used instead of names:
    - Tell Dad to call Sister.
    - Did you know Pastor is here?
    - Good morning, Team.
    - Right away, Boss!
    - Put Giraffe in the toy box.
    - I love you, Sweetheart.
- Words used to define regions, specific locations:
    - To drive to the South, you need to turn south onto Interstate 75.
    - The plane flew from the West Coast to New England.
    - The Ohio Valley experienced an early spring.
    - He biked from the Midwest to the West Coast.

Don't capitalize:

- Words that function as generic names
    - Tell my dad to call our sister.
    - Did you know the pastor is here?
    - Good morning to all on the team.
    - Right away! You're the boss!
    - Put your giraffe in the toy box.

- – I love you. You're my sweetheart.
- Words that function as general directions.
  - – John wanted to fly anywhere south to find warmer weather.
  - – The valley surrounding the Ohio River might flood.
  - – He biked west from the middle of the United States.

## 82. Capitalize Professional Titles that Precede Names.

When do we capitalize titles?

Capitalize when they precede the name:

- She is Superintendent Jane Archer
- He is State Senator John Green.
- Notify Chief Executive Officer Randi Smith is....

Don't capitalize when the title follows the name:

1. She is Jane Archer, the superintendent
2. He is John Green, the state senator from Michigan.
3. Notify Randi Smith, the chief executive officer is...

Exception: Acronyms:

4. Notify Randi Smith, the CEO is...

# 83. Books, Podcasts, Articles, etc.: What to Capitalize and How to Punctuate

The exceptions are prepositions (on, with, for, from, to, etc.) and articles (a, an, the).

Examples:

- The Good, the Bad, and the Ugly
- *To Kill a Mockingbird*
- *Return of the Jedi*
- *Harry Potter and the Goblet of Fire*
- "10 Tips for How to Grow Your Business Using Positive Communication"

The same preposition/article rule applies to job titles:

- Superintendent of Public Instruction Max Bennett visited our school.
- Secretary of State Mary Smith resigned.

When to italicize, underline, or parenthesize:

- Titles of books, movies, podcasts, and TV shows are italicized or underlined, as seen above. We italicize more often now that the function is readily available on computers.
- Titles of chapters in books, articles, and TV or podcast episodes are distinguished by quotation marks.

    Example:

    - In 1952, 71.9% of people who had television sets tuned into watch the *I Love Lucy* episode "Lucy Goes to the Hospital."

## 84. Capitalize the Name of Your Business, Club, Car, Boat, Cat, etc.

Capitalize the name of your business, organization, church, club, neighborhood association, car—I had a red Honda named Scarlet, dog, etc.

- Delta Airlines
- Fluffy
- The Backyard Club
- Riverside Neighborhood Association

Some businesses and organizations are now designing logos with their names written in all lower case. My opinion: They are doing it for artsy reasons and possibly to identify with their audience who has chosen not to capitalize when texting.

Using all-lower-case letters relegates those businesses and organizations to the category of common nouns—words such as cat, door, tree, plant—which diminishes their own importance for the sake of a logo. In my opinion, they are missing the opportunity to project an image of strength, expertise, and pride in their name.

Plus, they are playing loose with basic grammar rules, which frustrates all of us who were or are English teachers. It's difficult to teach proper nouns when students see businesses and organizations portray themselves as common nouns.

Okay. I've vented!

Where else do you see missed opportunities to capitalize?

# POLISHING YOUR WRITING

## 85. "est" and "er"

Best is not always better.

When comparing TWO persons, concepts, places, or things, the word to use is "better." Use "best" when comparing THREE or MORE.

This rule also applies to other words ending in "<u>er</u>" versus "<u>est.</u>"

Examples:

- Between options A and B, the better option is B; however, the best option is D.

- Jack is the older of the two sons and the oldest of all the children.

- Anna is taller than Rae. She is also the tallest in her class.

- The audience voted Derrik the funnier of the two finalists and the funniest comedian of the year.

- Lisa is the friendliest of all of our employees.

- We are accepting the lower bid of the two proposals.

- Make this a better week than last week...and the best week ever!

## 86. Use "to" Instead of "and" or "on."

Instead of using "on" or "and," use an infinitive ("to" + a verb).

Example:

- Avoid saying: "I'm planning on contacting the client."
- Say: "I'm planning to contact the client."

- Avoid saying: "I can try and pick up the lunch order."
- One option: "I can try to pick up the lunch order."

- Better option: "I can pick up the lunch order.
- Even better option: "I will be glad to pick up the lunch order."

Amazingly, the person saying, "I will be glad to....", which is an embedded positive command, actually feels glad to do it! The first time I said it, I felt more energetic, positive, and—yes—glad to fulfill the favor!

Bonus word awareness:

"Try" is a confidence-robbing word that sabotages the speaker's determination and tells others, "This isn't going to happen."

Whenever appropriate, replace "try" with strong verbs that produce results instead of excuses—words such as I "will" or "can."

## 87. Less, Much, and Amount Don't Count.

Use the words "less, much, and amount' if the next word is un-countable as these are:

- money, time, clothing, fog, fun, effort, boating, and traffic, etc.

Use the words "fewer, many, and number" if the word that follows is something you can count:

- dollars, hours, clothes, clouds, games, tasks, boats, and cars, etc.

Sentence examples:

- In spite of how <u>much</u> effort it took, and how <u>many</u> hours were involved, state police kept track of the <u>number</u> of vehicles to determine the <u>amount</u> of traffic using the dilapidated bridge.

- Because the magazine editor allocated <u>less</u> space, Alex had to use <u>fewer</u> words. The result: his more succinct story, which still contained as <u>much</u> information, attracted a larger-than-expected <u>number</u> of readers.

## 88. "Really" Does Not Mean "Very."

"Really" does not mean "very." They are not synonyms.

"Really" actually means truly or indeed. If you say, "The movie was really good." You are saying, "The movie was actually good."

Now...back to the word "very." I recommend my clients avoid it. "Very" allows the speaker/writer to mentally coast by selecting a favorite stand-by adjective and bolstering it with "very."

If the movie was more than very good, it might have been intriguing, spell-binding, cathartic, suspenseful, mesmerizing, life-changing, etc.

You will appreciate the effort and results of this more precise communication.

You really will.

## 89. What Kind of Verb Follows "or" or "nor:" Singular or Plural?

Singular or plural verb?

The words "or" or "nor" indicate you have a choice, and the noun or pronoun closest to the verb determines if the verb is singular or plural.

For example:

- Either the girls OR their PARENTS STAY.
- Neither the dogs NOR the CAT LIKES caviar.
- He guesses either his father OR his sisters ARE SINGING.
- Either the salespersons OR the BOSS HELPS me. (Your mind OR your EARS NEED to adjust to that one!)

## 90. **These Are Two Words — Not One**

Write them as two words — not one.

The words? "All right" and "a lot." (Instead of alright and alot.)

To remember this, think of the opposite: Would you write "alwrong" and "alittle?"

("Alright" is acceptable in informal writing; however, if you write a lot, you'll want to automatically default to the spelling that is all right all the time.)

## 91. Gerunds: Let's Own Them

Let's own our gerunds! (Stay with me!)

"Your smiling is contagious." In this sentence, we treat "smiling" as a noun. That's because it's a gerund, which is an "ing" form of a verb that functions as a noun.

Nouns can have modifiers — adjectives: In this case, the adjective is possessive: "your." (To whom does the smiling belong?) We could have used other possessive adjectives such as my, his, her, its, our, their, and whose.)

Why am I making this such a big deal? Because many people use pronouns (me, you, him us, them) instead.

Here is the correct and incorrect way to own your gerunds:

- My jogging up the stairs inspired her. Not: Me jogging...
- His snoring all night keeps me awake. Not: Him snoring...
- Our working overtime clinched it. Not: Us working...
- Their refusing to listen frustrated the boss. Not: Them refusing...
- Your reading this reinforces the concept. Not: You reading...

One more reinforcement: You wouldn't say, "Me presenting needs work. You would say "My presenting needs work." Now, enlarge that thought to include all gerunds and gerund phrases: "My presenting to small and large groups needs work."

My writing this tip and your wanting to learn it exemplify how our searching for growth continues.

Your using this correctly is another indication of your professionalism.

## 92. Use Apostrophes for Ownership, Not to Pluralize

Are you confused about pluralizing numbers or abbreviations? Treat them as traditional words—no apostrophes.

Examples of plurals:

- YMCAs, 1930s, VPs, 100s, PTAs
- CEOs in the 1990s retired in their 50s.

To show possession/ownership, treat numbers and abbreviations as words:

- The VP's vocabulary is similar to 1960's music lyrics.

The exception to the pluralization rule is making one letter plural. In that case, we do use apostrophes because they clear up confusion:

- Incorrect/confusing: "I'm striving for all as."
- Correct: "I'm striving for all a's."
- Incorrect/confusing: "I love the sound of long is."
- Correct: "I love the sound of long i's." (I actually do!)

And if you are among the increasing number of people who are inserting apostrophes to pluralize traditional words, please stop! What we all learned in first grade is still the rule:

- Correct: "The boys are here."
- Incorrect: "The boy's (or boys') are here."

## 93. **Misplaced Modifiers: Word Proximity Could Be Your Nemesis**

Word proximity can be your nemesis.

Double-check your word order. We don't want to confuse (and misinform) our readers.

For example:

- The jury convicted him for murdering her today. (This is, indeed, a speedy trial!)
- They kept a scrapbook of their children hidden in the closet. (Those children must have been cramped!)
- Luckily, the storm passed over us. (That's one lucky storm!)
- Randy was criticized by the boss because he was late. (The boss was late? Write instead: The boss criticized Randy because he was late)
- Seen on a furniture store sign: We have tables for families with thick legs.

Most of us accidentally misplace words in sentences, and that's why we need to re-read and correct what we write.

## 94. Searching for the Subject of the Sentence? Here's Where NOT to Look!

Where's the subject?

To discover the subject and easily see if you need a singular or plural verb, ignore all prepositional phrases between the subject and verb. (I've bracketed the propositional phrases below.)

Example:

- One [of the projects] is finished.

- The projects [for that company] are on schedule.

- [For ten minutes] [before all the meetings], Bill, [without his co-workers], walks the halls.

- The employee [with the skills] [over all the interns] deserves a bonus.

- Prepositional phrases, [if they are non-essential], are separated by commas. That's another clue!

Look again at the examples and notice which prepositional phrases are non-essential—and are, therefore, separated by commas.

## 95. Prepositions at the End of Sentences? Yes and No.

To simplify construction and meaning, grammar decision-makers (that's a book in itself!) have relaxed this no-prepositions-at-the-end-of-sentences rule.

However, not all sentences that end in prepositions are easier to understand. Here is an example:

- A preposition is something you may want to avoid ending a sentence with.
- Simply stated:
- You may want to avoid ending sentences with prepositions.

With this in mind, all of these examples below are acceptable:

- Who is that for?
- For whom is that?

- What speaker did you learn that from?
- From what speaker did you learn that?
- (or you can ask: Who taught you that?)

- What reason did you ask that for?
- For what reason did you ask that?
- (or you can ask: Why did you ask that?)

One preposition rule does remain. Eliminate *needless* prepositions tagged on at the end of sentences.

Examples:

- Where is he going to? (Say: "Where is he going?")
- Where does she live at? (Say: "Where does she live?")

## PUNCTUATIONS: WHERE AND WHEN TO USE

### 96. Bullet Points

Bullet points are essential. I use them liberally, and I encourage you to do the same.

Bullet points make writing and reading easier and faster. They:

- Organize the material visually for you and your readers.
- Simplify the message.
- Create more white space.

Here's an indispensable rule you'll appreciate knowing: All bullet points need to begin with the same word group — nouns, adverbs, gerunds, verbs, etc. The bullet points above all begin with verbs:

Notice all the bullet points in the example above use "they" as their lead in. In making "they" the introductory phrase, I reduce the number of words and start each bullet point with the key words — the verbs. If we add "they" to every line, we create redundancy and de-emphasize the key words.

- They organize...
- They simplify...
- They create...

Here are more examples of bullet points beginning with other word groups:

- (nouns) The boss wants each of us to bring the following:

- notebooks
- pencils
- calendars
- budgets

- (gerunds) This is Tom's idea of a perfect day:
  - sleeping in
  - reading
  - eating lunch with friends
  - watching football

One more rule: If the information delineated by bullet points contains sentences, you punctuate them as sentences. Here is an example:

- (verbs) To ensure your email recipients read your emails, do the following to create more white space:
  - Double space between paragraphs.
  - Increase the number of paragraphs. Create a new one every time a topic changes—even slightly.
  - Use bullet points when you need to make several points.

If you want tasks prioritized of completed in chronological order, use numbers.

- (verbs) This is our plan for the banquet:
  1. Set up the chairs and tables.
  2. Serve the food.
  3. Clean up afterward.
  4. Return the key.

You are now bullet point certified! Go out and amaze your colleagues!

## 97. **Brackets**

(Clearing up the [bracket] confusion.) What is their purpose?

Let's start with their name:

What we call "brackets" in American English are called "square brackets" in other English-speaking countries. That's because people in those countries call parentheses "brackets."

Why use brackets? They:

- enclose words added by someone other than the original writer or speaker, typically...to clarify the situation: *
    - She [the defendant] hysterically ran out of the courtroom.
- function as parentheses within parentheses:
    - The world-changing punctuation document (covered with dust in the [dilapidated] historical museum) is worth millions.

On the topic of punctuation, if brackets — and parentheses — are used at the end of sentences, the final punctuations are placed after them:

- She told me she loved "Mr. Squeeze" [her python].
- "Draw near to God, and He will draw near to you" (James 4:8).

*Oxford Living Dictionaries

## 98. Hyphens between Words

Solving the mind-paralyzing hyphenating conundrum.

We hyphenate two or more words that describe a noun they precede if those words have teamed up to act as a single word. Hyphenating physically connects them to create one word.

Because these connected words do the work of one adjective, they are called, appropriately, compound adjectives.

This is a frustratingly-confusing and, consequently, often-ignored hyphenating rule. That's because the rule only applies to words that precede the noun. (frustratingly-confusing and often-ignored modify rule.)

If those same words follow the noun they modify (rule), they are not hyphenated. So, not only is this rule frustratingly confusing and often ignored, it can also be confusing.

To summarize:

- These words are hyphenated because they precede the nouns they modify:
    - The seven-toed dog won the animal-lovers' competition.
    - The follow-up email needs to be succinct.
- These words are not hyphenated because they follow the nouns they modify:
    - The dog with seven toes won the competition attended by animal lovers.
    - The email you send to follow up needs to be succinct.
    - When you follow up, do it succinctly.

- Oh, and these words are always hyphenated:
    - self-control, self-centered, self-esteem (all words that begin with "self")
    - mother-in-law, father-in-law, president-elect, editor-in-chief, ex-husband, ex-wife,

    Find more examples on the internet.

Congratulations! You have now achieved the always-confident stage of hyphenating.

## 99. Commas, Periods, and Question Marks: Inside or Outside?

Question marks? Periods. Exclamation points! Do they go inside or outside the quotation marks?

In the U.S., periods and commas go inside the quotation marks:

- Alex said, "Yes, I will exercise the night away."

In the U.K., periods and commas go outside the quotation marks:

- Alex said, "Yes, I will exercise the night away".

Back to the U.S.: Question marks and exclamation points go inside the quotation marks if the quoted words comprise only a part of the question:

- Did Alex just say he's going to "exercise the night away"?

Single quotation marks: We use them when we have a quote within a quote:

- Sam said, "Emma was surprised Alex said he 'will exercise the night away.'"

My response to Alex: "Good luck finding party-goers willing to do that!"

<u>Bonus punctuation gem:</u>

Use semi-colons to separate phrases that already contain commas. Semi-colons are stronger punctuations and take over the job of separating when needed:

Example:

- The boss wants us to first, be on time; next, meet him in the boardroom; and finally, be prepared.

## THE FINISHING TOUCHES

### 100. Double Check Spell Check

Spell Check is intuitive; it is also fallible. For that reason, we need to scrutinize its results to ensure our minds — and not spell check's rendition of our minds — control our documents' content.

I learned this lesson a few years ago. I had written, proofread, and re-read an email to a company CEO; and right before I signed it, I typed "Conscientiously Yours" as my complimentary close. In my rush to send the email, I misspelled "Conscientiously." Spell check caught it, I glanced at the correction, and I quickly accepted it. After all, it started with "con" and ended with "tiously," and it was the length of the word I wanted.

After signing my name, I copied a colleague in the office, and sent the email. A few seconds later, I heard the colleague mutter, "This is strange." I instinctively knew that my quick decision was a wrong one! I rushed to his computer, looked at my email, and realized I had chosen "Contentiously Yours."

I immediately called the CEO and explained that in my quest to compliment him, I insulted him! The CEO — a person with whom I had a good relationship — laughed at the irony and graciously dismissed the situation. I, however, silently vowed never to be too busy to READ what I select with spell check – every syllable!

That was my fault; however, spell check has a few idiosyncrasies of its own: Many times, it defaults to the wrong you're/your. You need to know the correct word.

The same goes for making words plural. Simple procedure, right? Just add an "s." However, some spell checks add an apostrophe before the "s"

It's ironic that we have to check the accuracy of the software created so we can spell accurately!

# 101. Proofread and Find a Proofreader.

We need two sets of eyes!

<u>Our eyes</u>:

When we complete our emails, blogs, texts, we need to read them several times for continuity, spelling, and editing. It's during those times that we eliminate those extraneous, negative, confusion-causing words and sentence constructions.

<u>Someone else's eyes</u>:

Regardless of your expertise, if you're composing important emails or documents, have at least one other person read what you wrote before you send or publish them.

How many times have you repeatedly read your completed documents and emails and didn't see the missing words, repeated words, misspelled words, unnecessary words, dangling modifiers, or inaccuracies? That's right: You didn't SEE them! (And in some cases, you SAW words, but they actually weren't there!) Our minds know what we intend to communicate and think we accomplished that.

You may be just starting to sharpen your verbal edge with these communication skills and know you would benefit from someone coaching you and routinely proofreading all of your documents for a while. Go for it!

Teachability and vulnerability are qualities leaders possess. People admire other people who want to improve their skills. And those who are asked to coach or proofread feel honored to do so. I know. I am a coach, I've had business coaches, and I routinely ask people to critique my writing. The results are so worth it!

(My husband read this tip before I originally posted it. I ask him to read all of my tips before I post them. As for this book: A good friend, my husband, and an editor proofread this manuscript before I sent it to the publisher.)

The more people seek and find coaches, seminars, people, articles, and books to enhance their skills, the more equipped and confident they become.

Thank you for reading this book and putting the tips into action. Please contact me if you would like some personal coaching or workshops for your teams. Also, please also contact me to share how something in this book changed your life—professionally or personally. I would consider that your gift to me!

God bless you and your endeavors. I'm glad you made the decision to *Sharpen Your Verbal Edge!*

# Acknowledgments

I am grateful to the following people who each played a role—whether they know it or not—in this book and its contents becoming a reality.

My thanks to Craig Crook, friend and president of ReThink. Craig jump-started everything! He challenged me to increase the number of tips I posted and held me accountable for that. Motivated, I watched my occasionally-scheduled tips amass into an abundance of regularly-scheduled tips that readers anticipated.

Thank you, Communication Tip Readers. You are the reason I've compiled these tips into this book. My thanks to you who have loyally read them over the years and to you who have recently discovered them. Thank you for the value you place on them, your interest, your comments, and your partnering with me to suggest future tips.

I am grateful to Daryle Doden, CEO of Ambassador Enterprises and former president of Ambassador Steel Corporation. Daryle Doden invested in me and told me to "follow my dream." Daryle is a friend, former boss, and highly successful entrepreneur who speaks his mind. As a result of his telling me to follow my dreams, founded The Verbal Edge and, as a result, have written this book that will equip readers worldwide with professional skills previously available only to my clients. I will always be grateful to Daryle for this trajectory-changing advice.

Paul Saalfield and Steve Kucharski also deserve recognition. They are members of a weekly mastermind group and they relentlessly urged me for years to widen the scope of the people I reach. Paul is a successful entrepreneur and an award-winning Century 21 Bradley Realtor and Steve is an avid reader and a goal-inspiring, community-involved Raymond James financial advisor. I admire both men and thank them for continuing to push me to accomplish this next step. I thank them for being such good examples and for keeping this endeavor top of my mind.

My gratitude to TG Publishing's Lil Barcaski who kept me on track and guided me to organize my random communication tips into a structured format.

I am indebted to life-long friend and attorney Jane Gerardot for putting aside three days to proofread and edit the book's final manuscript. I told her to "Bring it on!" And she did! What a thorough job! Our grade school teachers would be proud of the careers we've built anchored by the English/grammar skills they masterfully implanted.

Thanks to my Verbal Edge mentor and advisor Karl LaPan, president and CEO of the Northeast Indiana Innovation Center, Inc. Over the years, Karl has explained best practices, helped clarify my goals, encouraged my more ambitious goals, and continues to support me with his can-do attitude. This book is a result of what he's taught me, poured into me, and exemplified.

My thanks to the following people who have encouraged, taught, and inspired me:

159

- Jim Bradley, president of and CEO of Century 21 Bradley
- John Richards, president of Solution Frameworks Consulting
- Irene Walters, community leader, former executive director of IPFW's university relations, and former Verbal Edge board member
- Kathy Carrier, president of Briljent LLC and former Verbal Edge board member
- Mary Popovitch, business advisor for the Indiana Small Business Development Center
- Bill Causey, entrepreneur and SCORE mentor

I am grateful to the extraordinary corporate and non-profit clients who have partnered with me to customize workshops and consultations. They have stretched me as much or more than I have stretched them.

Thank you to my daughters Kristi MacDonald and Kate High and my son-in-law Zach High who appreciate (put up with?) my passion for words, vocabulary building, and championing correct grammar. Thank you, also, to Tanzania Suliman and Talisha McCurrie who became part of our family for a season, and who eagerly lived this communication-focused life with us.

My husband Greg MacDonald deserves so much recognition! He has supported me in every facet of my transition from TV broadcasting to equipping others with communication skills. That transition involved my starting a business, hours and days of researching and creating workshops, years of writing and posting communication tips, and weeks devoted to writing this book. Throughout my professional journey, Greg made it a priority to listen, share his insights, proofread my communication tips, and be available to answer questions and share his wisdom. I am able to achieve so many dreams and goals because of the man the Lord gave me.

And I give thanks and praise to the Lord whom I felt beside me all along. I asked for his involvement, and that involvement was palpable! I was continually amazed and humbled that God, the Creator and Ruler of Heaven and the Universe, prompted me to spot mistakes when I wasn't looking for them, inspired me with words and ideas, and made the process of writing this book smooth and enjoyable. To you, Lord, be the glory.

# About the Author

Elizabeth (Liza) MacDonald is a corporate communication advisor, consultant, and owner of The Verbal Edge. Located in Fort Wayne, Indiana and the Tampa Bay area, The Verbal Edge equips individuals and groups to speak, write, and interact, and present themselves positively and with confidence.

Through workshops and individual consultations, Elizabeth partners with her clients to achieve desired skills and to detect and eliminate communication challenges.

Elizabeth's professional background includes

- TV reporting, anchoring, talk-show hosting, and producing
- Marketing and communications for Fort Wayne, Indiana Community Schools
- Teaching high school English.

She graduated from Indiana University at Fort Wayne with a B.S. in Education--focusing on sociology, history and English. Elizabeth completed her master's degree coursework and graduate orals in Broadcast Communication at San Francisco State University.